Arthur Herzog

THE
SWARM

SIMON AND SCHUSTER · NEW YORK

SBN 671-21709-7
LIBRARY OF CONGRESS CATALOG CARD NUMBER: 73-16476
DESIGNED BY EVE METZ
MANUFACTURED IN THE UNITED STATES OF AMERICA

1 2 3 4 5 6 7 8 9 10

ACKNOWLEDGMENTS

This book could not have been written without the generous help of the following organizations and individuals:

National Academy of Sciences; U.S. Army, Fort Detrick, Maryland; U.S. Department of Agriculture; Zoecon Corporation, Palo Alto, California.

Dr. John Perkins and Messrs. Howard Lewis, Bradley Byers and Martin Shepherd, NAS; Drs. Marshall Levin and Reese Sailer, USDA; Drs. T. S. K. Johansson and Robert Calhoon, Queens College, New York; Dr. Paul Hurd, Smithsonian Institution; Dr. Norman Coleman, Allergy Foundation of America; Dr. Robert Brooks, Jr., Fairfax Radiation Facility; Dr. Vincent Dole, Rockefeller University, New York; Dr. Roger Morse, Cornell University; Dr. Joan Ehrenfeld, Museum of Natural History, New York City; Dr. Michael Baden, Deputy Coroner, City of New York; Dr. Ron Sederoff, Columbia University; Ms. Sheila Pack; Dr. James A. Gilford, Hood College, Maryland; Mr. John E. Patton, a "ham."

At Fort Detrick, Mr. E. P. Magaha, Public Affairs Officer; Mr. Charles Crum, U.S. Army Health Services Data Systems Agency; Mr. Orley R. Bourland, Jr., National Cancer Institute; Dr. Lynn H. Wright, Litton Bionetics, Inc.; Captain Allan W. Deware, Signal Corps; Captain David T. O'Conner, Sergeant

5

First Class Arthur Beverly and Staff Sergeant John W. Daugherty, U.S. Army Strategic Communications Command, East Coast Telecommunications Center.

I wish to thank them all for their willingness to share their expertise. My special thanks to Perkins, an environmental biologist; Johansson, biologist and bee man extraordinary; Brooks, a physiologist; and Levin, an entomologist. All made invaluable technical suggestions and went over the manuscript. And my gratitude to Mack Magaha, who saw to it that Fort Detrick was mine.

For the encouragement of my editor, Phyllis Grann, I shall always be grateful.

FOR MATTHEW
WHEN HE GROWS UP

CONTENTS

9

The bee's sustained flight, its powerful sting, its intimacy with flowers and avoidance of all unwholesome things, the attachment of the workers to the queen—regarded throughout antiquity as the king—its singular swarming habits and its astonishing industry in collecting and storing honey and skill in making wax, two unique substances of great value to man, but of mysterious origin, made it a divine being, a prime favorite of the gods, that had somehow survived the golden age or had voluntarily escaped from the garden of Eden with poor fallen man for the purpose of sweetening his bitter lot.

W. M. WHEELER, *Social Life Among the Insects*

BEE-STING DEATHS IN AFRICA ON RISE
Local Strain More Vicious than European Variety

JOHANNESBURG, South Africa (Reuters)—Bees are becoming a serious danger in South Africa.

One naturalist calculates that swarms of angry bees have caused more deaths during the last decade in this country than any other form of wild life—including lions and snakes. [*New York Times,* May 8, 1966]

DEADLY BEES ATTACK AFRICAN MARCHERS:
BOY IS BADLY STUNG

MARYKNOLL, N.Y.—A strange story of a deadly assault by a swarm of bees on a Palm Sunday procession has been reported by Sister Rose Leon, a nurse and one of the Maryknoll Sisters stationed in Shinyonga, Tanzania, a small town not far from Lake Victoria.

"The procession of Christians was advancing across the fields toward the church," the sister related, "when a swarm of bees attacked us.

"The hundreds of people screamed and ran.

"One little crippled boy on crutches fell and the bees descended upon him. He screamed and screamed. At least six men tried to carry him but were bitten so badly they dropped him and ran away themselves. . . ." [*Religious News Service,* May 27, 1966]

VICIOUS BEES TERRIFY SOUTH AFRICANS:
5 KILLED BY STINGS

JOHANNESBURG, South Africa—Notoriously vicious bees, apparently irritated more than usual by hot weather, have terrified South Africans with angry attacks in the last six months.

Five people were stung to death. Hundreds of others suffered painful stings. Pet dogs and other animals died in the onslaught.

People fleeing in panic before swarms of bees in several cases dived into swimming pools or public fountains to escape the invaders. [*Knickerbocker News,* Albany, June 1, 1966]

ENTOMOLOGY
Danger from the African Queens

Apiculturist Warwick Kerr figured he had some perfectly good reasons for bringing 20 African queen bees into his native Brazil nine years ago. Though it is known to be ferocious, the African bee produces 30 percent more honey than either the Italian or German bee that long dominated Brazilian beekeeping. Besides, Kerr planned to crossbreed his Africans to produce a more gentle bee. What he got instead was a bee with a disposition so nasty that it now threatens the lives and livelihood of almost every beekeeper in eight states of Brazil—to say nothing of countless other Brazilians. [*Time*, Sept. 24, 1965]

PERU WAGES DRIVE ON BEES

LIMA, Peru, June 15 (Reuters)—Emergency measures are being taken here to prevent an invasion of deadly African bees from Brazil, the Agrarian Defense Directorate said today. [*New York Times*, June 16, 1968]

DREAD AFRICAN BEE ACOMIN'?
THIS BREED WON'T BUZZ OFF

WASHINGTON (UPI)—Evil-tempered bees that sting man and beast for the apparent pleasure of causing pain threaten to invade North America.

The African bees migrated from their native land to Brazil in 1956 and spread rapidly over an area about equal to the continental United States.

The warning about a possible invasion northward came from Dr. M. J. Ramsay, a research scientist at the Agriculture Department. He announced that $40,000 in contingency funds will be made available—at the urgent request of the American Beekeeping Federation—to study the problem and see what can be done to prevent its spread into Central and North America. [*Miami Herald*, Tues., July 20, 1971]

14

INVASION BY AGGRESSIVE HONEYBEES IS FELT
By Boyce Rensberger

A vast army of fierce African honeybees, the descendants of 26 swarms accidentally released in Brazil 15 years ago, has spread through much of South America and threatens eventually to invade North America, a committee of experts commissioned by the National Academy of Sciences has found.

The African bees, a strain of the species common to the Americas, are virtually identical to the American variety in appearance but quite different in behavior. They are much more aggressive and more likely to attack in swarms. [*New York Times*, Jan. 22, 1972]

Brazil Menace
KILLER BEES ARE HEADING FOR U.S.

WASHINGTON (AP)—Swarms of ferocious honeybees that have been known to kill both humans and animals are moving toward the United States from Brazil at the rate of 200 miles a year.

There seems to be no natural barrier to block the bees, and they could be in North America within four to six years, says a study financed by the Agriculture Department.

"The most alarming and best-known characteristic of Brazilian bees is their aggressiveness," according to the report. [*Chicago Daily News*, Aug. 24, 1972]

PART ONE

The
African Queens

1

A PICNIC

Several facts concerning the incident near Maryville, New York, need to be underscored.

The day was unusually warm for late September.

Asters, goldenrod and other late-blooming flowers grew in profusion.

There were picnickers—a family named Peterson—whose provisions included sugar in various forms; as it turned out, too much sugar for their own good.

Taking full advantage of the weather, wild bees were frantically gathering nectar and pollen before winter descended and shut off their supply until spring.

Leaving their car on the road, the Petersons struggled with their picnic things through the woods: Bill, stout and genial; Mary, small and wiry; the children, Karen, twelve, Tim, ten, Randy, six—all blond and big for their ages. The family discovered they had the spot to themselves. A copse of soft maples, alders and willlows opened into a grassy clearing that ended at a small stream. Birds babbled and insects strummed.

The children played, and Bill, sprawled in a camp chair, listened to a ball game on the radio. Mary, who wanted the sun, undid the top buttons of her blouse and smeared herself with sweet-smelling skin lotion. Her skin was pale. All summer long the meteorological pattern had been the same: hot and sunny on weekdays, rainy on weekends—marvelous for things that grow, but terrible for people.

When lunchtime came, Bill stretched a tarp on the grass and set up the card table. They had been in a hurry to leave, and Mary let them throw what they liked into the picnic box. She frowned at the nutritional catastrophe that had been assembled. Hamburgers, hot dogs, buns, condiments, leftover pizza, potato chips, pretzels, cheese wafers, Slim Jims, macaroni salad, powdered doughnuts, marshmallows, Crackerjacks, nuts, candy, Oreos, Fig Newtons, cupcakes, soft drinks . . .

Someone had built a crude fireplace with rocks. Bill shook in charcoal, squirted a runnel of fluid and lit a match. White smoke rose straight up. Karen and Tim were throwing the ball just over little Randy's head, but soon the kids arrived at the table with their mouths open, like young birds. Always the greediest, Karen grabbed the potato chips, attacked the cellophane package with her teeth and inserted grubby fingers. Mary yanked the bag away, but the situation was already out of hand. Tim had ripped the top from the Crackerjack box, and Randy had expertly torn the tab from a can of Coke. "You kids," sighed Mary. "I give up."

"Can I have some honey, Mother?" Karen asked. "Honey is good for you. It gives you energy." The question was a formality. Without waiting for an answer she smeared butter on a bun and held the jar upside down until honey gushed tawnily.

"Troops won't wait, Bill," Mary called. "My, it *is* buggy today." She took the aerosol can and shot a warning burst of insecticide at the bushes.

When the coals glowed under mantles of white ash, Bill put the bright red patties stippled with fat on the grill, pressing each with his spatula. He ordered a phalanx of franks. Around the edges of the grill he laid the pale faces of the buns. Holding a beer, he sat on his haunches and watched the falling fat erupt into tiny flames.

He had just turned the burgers when Karen discovered the bee. She had forgotten to put the lid on the jar, and when she clapped it down the bee was a prisoner on the glass wall. "I caught a bee!"

Tim ran up. "That's a big bee." It was the size of a large marble, black with rows of tufted orange hair on its rear section. "Maybe it's a bumblebee."

"It's a honeybee," Karen said firmly. "We had a beehive in a glass box at school." She showed the bee to her mother.

Mary stared at it apprehensively. She didn't know much about bees, but it looked enormous to her. "Maybe it's a queen."

"Queen bees don't just fly *around*, Mother," Karen said. "They only fly to mate."

Randy wanted to inspect the bee too. He snatched the jar from Karen's hands and ran a few steps with it. The bee came to life. From inside the jar it made a startlingly loud noise, almost like a growl, high-pitched and sharp as a sting. *Zeeeeeeeee. Ziiiiiiii.* The buzz frightened Randy, who let the honey-slick jar slip from his fingers. It shattered on a log and the bee escaped. Furious, crying, Randy began to kick the log.

"Stay away from the glass," Bill ordered. "We'll clean up later. Chow's on."

The parents sat in their camp chairs while the kids sprawled on the tarp, holding up their plastic plates and Styrofoam cups for more. They had reached the ice cream–cookie–marshmallow stage when Tim noticed a dozen bees congregated around the shards of the honey jar. More bees prowled around the little pile of rubbish the kids had thrown on the grass near the tarp. Every now and then a bee rose in the air and flew like a dart toward the trees. Bravely, Tim tried to shoo the bees away, but they buzzed queerly and gave no ground.

Bees circled over the table too, hovering over the powdered doughnuts and Fig Newtons, retreating, returning, coming ever closer.

"I don't like these bees," Mary said. She stood up, took her magazine and sat on the grass by the stream, determined to enjoy the day. Bill moved his chair and radio away from the table, while the children threw a Frisbee. The clearing seemed to throb like a living tissue with the hum of insects.

Mary looked up and saw that her youngest child was scurrying toward her, jerking his head and arms in an unnatural way. He cried, "A bee is chasing me!"

Mary got up quickly and went to him. "They're just bees, Randy. They won't hurt you if you don't hurt them," she said. The boy threw his face convulsively against her stomach while, inches away, a bee zoomed by, screaming like a tiny jet fighter.

Following it with her eyes, she saw that the table was crowded with bees running over the food with stiff legs. Mary inched closer. "They're into everything," she whispered. "Those are just not natural bees."

At her side, Karen said in a small voice, "I thought bees ate only pollen and nectar. Those bees are pigs, just like us kids."

"I don't get it," Mary said, watching the bees crawl on the sweet things, seeming even to scrape at the Styrofoam cups in their hunger. She dared to snatch the insecticide can from the table, jabbed the button and held it down until her thumb was white from the pressure. "Go way! Go way, bees!" she yelled.

The bees appeared to go crazy. They rose and fell, swirled in the air, rolled in bunches on the ground. A few bees hurled themselves into the white-hot charcoal, exploding like little shells. Above, the bee cloud grew. With its angry fringes and turbulent center, it looked like a miniature storm.

Hunched over the radio as he listened to an important play, Bill was oblivious to everything. "Goddammit, Daddy," Mary said sharply, "turn off the radio. Let's get out of here."

22

Bill switched off the radio. When he did, it became apparent that the radio, instead of causing, had only masked the true source of the noise in the clearing. A roar like a chain saw in operation rose from the bushes, the trees, the very ground. The Petersons raised shocked faces—the sky was black with bees.

"Leave the picnic things," Mary shrieked. "Children, run!"

Randy raced for the car, while Tim headed for the stream. Karen screamed, "A bee's in my hair!" and with frantic gestures tried to pull it out. She screamed again. As if she had been touched by fire, a sharp weal rose abruptly on her neck. The sound in the clearing changed, almost resembling a deep organ note. *Zuuuuuuuuuummmmm.* Bees swooped from the sky. Bill's hand shot to his arm, then to his shoulder. He dropped the radio.

Mary was running toward them, but wavered and stopped, confused by the whirling shadows and hideous sound. ZUUUUUUUUUMMMMM. Bees brushed all over her, on her arms, down her cleavage, even flying under her skirt. Desperately she tried to brush them away, but a hundred lances seemed to punch everywhere into her body. Her eyelids puffed and her nostrils began to close. A strange aching filled her chest and breath came hard. She opened her mouth to scream but received on her tongue a swab of pain. As she fell, she asked herself what would become of the children.

2

THE NATIONAL ACADEMY

On Monday the warm weather continued down the eastern sea-board. It was 70 degrees by 8 A.M., according to the radio. Dr. John Wood decided to bike to work.

Over breakfast Wood had a characteristic debate with him-self. His companion of the night before, a pert young woman, had departed earlier while he slept. She was the latest in a long series of women who had given up on Wood. They liked him well enough—too much, it seemed; the trouble had to do with the time he had for them—namely, little. Between women and work Wood always chose the latter, neglecting the former, whose reactions were then predictable. "Must learn to relax and play more," Wood told himself for the nth time. Then, as usual, the day swallowed him up.

In Wood's scientific circles there was nothing unusual in the fact that his bike, a three-hundred-dollar Peugeot with ten gears and centerfold brakes, was worth as much as his car, an old Volks. After parking the bicycle in the garage he climbed the stairs to the Great Hall, with its green-bronze portals decorated with the signs of the zodiac, pillars of green Italian marble, elaborately domed ceiling, and the painting of "Prometheus Bound" on the far wall. Wanting a temple to the Great God Science, they had built one. The National Academy of Sciences was the sort of place that called a courtyard an arboretum and its cafeteria a refectory. The temple was implacably, irretrievably sedate. Sometimes Wood wished it provided a bit more action.

As usual, *The Washington Post* stared from his desk, where the divisional secretary left it each morning. Wood stared back at it with something nearing real dislike. He had a theory that newspapers were owned by pharmaceutical companies and printed expressly to increase the sales of tranquilizers. The trouble was that the papers got people stirred up about all the wrong things, ignoring the ones that mattered. Wood always put off reading the paper as long as he could, and sometimes happily forgot to read it at all. Today, with fifteen minutes yawning before his Monday meeting with Hubbard, he had no excuse.

He was an inveterate reader of the colorful filler items at the bottoms of pages, which often interested him more than the major news: "Sea Lion Gives Birth to Quints"; "Femme-Lib Wife Jails Hubby on Alimony Rap." His eyes stopped at a small headline.

FAMILY ATTACKED BY BEES—TWO KILLED

MARYVILLE, N.Y., Sept. 26 (AP)—A family of five on an outing in an isolated spot by a stream were attacked by bees here.

Mr. and Mrs. William Peterson died as the result of bee bites. Their three children were also attacked, one, Karen, age 12, severely.

The local coroner, Dr. David P. Znac, speculated that both adults had allergies to bee bites, which can be fatal. About 30 deaths a year in the U.S. are attributed to bites from bees, wasps and hornets.

What caused the bees to attack is not known.

Wood's characteristic reaction to information that troubled him was to back away from it temporarily and give his intuition a chance to operate. Also, at that moment he felt a surge of very real fear. His only immediate response concerned the reporter's ignorance. Bees don't bite, he thought, they sting, as he himself had good cause to remember. He worked quickly to the end of the paper, then found himself studying the bee item more closely.

Wood was not an entomologist, much less a bee man. But he was an environmental biologist with knowledge in many areas, including a bit of melittology, and to him the facts presented had an odd ring. A mass attack indicated honeybees, not solitary bees, but honeybees don't usually swarm so late in the year. Still, it had been hot. Wood's impression (an erroneous one, it turned out, though shared by many others) was that most bees lived in beeyards, so what were they doing out in the wilds? And, he believed, the chance of two people in the same family having fatal anaphylactic reactions to bee stings was small.

But what bothered Wood most was that mass attacks by honeybees were extremely rare, except in the case of one singular bee race. On impulse, Wood clipped and filed the article.

Wood served at the National Academy as Chief Staff Officer of the Division of Environmental Sciences. Sheldon Hubbard, the Executive Officer, was his boss. Every Monday the two men met to review the work of their unit, which acted as a kind of troubleshooter, trying to spot environmental crises before they arose. Entering Hubbard's office, Wood found it empty and was glad. The bee killings had upset him. He wanted a minute to calm down.

Shelly Hubbard's personality reached out from the office walls—wife, kids, dog, degrees, honorary degrees, photos of Hubbard with Willard Lightower, the Academy's president, with Soviet scientists, receiving the Pudlo Award for distinguished zoological research, shooting a rifle, grinning over a golf trophy. He was a many-faceted scientist and his lush talents spread from machinery to military history. He was also an egomaniac, whose biggest disappointment was to have failed to achieve international renown.

Wood's liking for the older scientist did not blind him to Hubbard's shortcomings. As a bureaucrat Hubbard could be slow to act, reluctant to change course, prideful and stubborn. He let his ego get in the way and had too much confidence in his own judgment. To Wood, Hubbard's real talent was innovation. He should have remained a bench scientist, Wood thought, and not yielded to the flimsy attraction of power his job offered.

Hubbard's attitude toward the younger scientist, with whom he had a good-natured rivalry, was not completely favorable either. He called Wood (along with the generation of younger scientists he represented) a mere calculating machine—sharp, shrewd, cool, but without blood or bile. Wood knew this description contained some truth.

Fifteen minutes late, as usual, Shelly Hubbard bustled in. To Wood, Hubbard resembled his own zoological specialty, the beetle. At fifty-two he was short and massively broad, with a bulging chest. He had almost no neck at all, and his round head seemed to pivot directly on his sloping shoulders. Two fringes of black hair stood up on the sides of his bald dome like antennae. Habitually, and in line with his coleoptera character, Hubbard rubbed his hands together with a rustling sound or created sucking noises by making a vacuum between his palms.

Hubbard dropped weightily into a chair at the conference table across from Wood, surveying the pile of work before them balefully. Wood asked him about the weekend golf. Hubbard made a face and said he had shot in the low 90s. Then Hubbard asked, "Hey, could you fill in for me at the entomological society this week, John? I'd rather play golf. I've had meetings to here." He placed his hand on the top of his bald head.

"Sure," Wood said. "I want to talk to Gerston anyway."

"Good. Those new results of his are the scariest thing since Frankenstein's monster. Speaking of which, we have a few in the deck this morning."

A foot high, the pile consisted of evaluations, proposals,

strategies, requests from government agencies and the like, with Wood's recommendations stapled to each. The first was a report prepared by a group of southern scientists, destined for the U.S. Department of Agriculture. It said that the canary-winged parakeet and the Amazon parrot, both of which had been accidentally released in Florida, posed a serious threat to fruit crops. The scientists recommended immediate action. Wood had said yes; Hubbard said yes, and the proposal was cleared for the Academy's Program Review Committee.

The next item concerned "superrat," as British newspapers called it jokingly. Knowledgeable scientists hardly thought superrat a joke. Rats, like other animals, had developed resistance to conventional poisons; then an anticoagulant called warfarin had been developed which caused rats to bleed internally and die. Here, scientists thought, was a poison to which no resistance was possible, and yet, a few generations later, rats became resistant to warfarin too. Warfarin-resistant rats had even been found in upstate New York. But the British warfarin-resistant rat had taken a further evolutionary jump. As though it thrived on the poisons used against it, it had become about one-fourth larger than ordinary rats and could chew through plaster walls. Stories (unsubstantiated) had it that superrat would stand up to a cat or small dog and fight to the death. Whether or not these reports were true, no doubt existed about the rat's aggressiveness.

Now the Environmental Protection Agency wanted a study on what to do about superrat if it ever reached American cities. In crowded ghetto areas it could cause havoc.

Hubbard shuddered. "I have a thing about rats. Remember what Orwell said in *1984*—that everybody has one thing he is afraid of? In the book there was a prisoner who seemed unafraid of anything, and they put a cage on his head with a hungry rat in it. He broke. Just the suggestion of rats has that effect on me."

Wood was totally unmoved by rats. He wondered idly if rats ate beetles. "One thing I'm curious about," he said, "is why suddenly increased size seems to lead to heightened aggressiveness. That's been observed in insects too. Could the same be true of man? We're growing larger."

But Hubbard seemed eager to change the subject. "Give that proposal top priority. Send it direct to Lightower." He made the squishing noise with his hands.

In this way they inched through the stack with Hubbard giving assent to almost everything Wood proposed. Later Wood was to speculate on what might have happened in the matter of the African bees if Hubbard hadn't stubbornly wished to prove to Wood that he was still capable of saying no, and if the McAllister proposal hadn't been near the end of the pile, when Hubbard always grew restless. Nothing different, surely. Still, it was tempting to wonder whether a few vital weeks might have been saved.

F. W. McAllister, apiologist, or bee man, from Kansas University and a member of the National Academy, had been part of the team sent by the Academy to Brazil a few years earlier to study the African honeybee and write a report.* This bee presented something of a puzzle. It was undeniably vigorous. Compared with the bees of European descent that populate the Americas, it got out earlier in the morning, worked harder during the day, and stayed out later in the evening. For this reason it was capable of producing almost twice as much honey as the bees of the Americas. But it was also extremely aggressive and prone to unprovoked mass attacks on humans and livestock. It had a high rate of reproduction, and because of the crowding that followed, swarmed frequently and at great distances. It liked to live in the wilds.

In 1956 a Brazilian entomologist had imported African bees

* Final Report, Committee on the African Honey Bee, Division of Biology and Agriculture, National Academy of Sciences, Washington, D.C., June 1972.

with the idea of crossbreeding them with Brazilian bees and creating a bee family as industrious as the Africans but as docile as the European bee. The first lot of African bees had been carefully selected for gentleness, but it had been sprayed with DDT en route and arrived in Brazil dead. Rumor said that the second lot of African bees had been collected at random, without regard to screening out the more vicious ones. At any rate, the bees arrived in Brazil. Before the crossbreeding experiments were completed an unbelievable series of errors resulted in the escape of twenty-six swarms headed by African queens. Entomologists had been sure that the aggressive African gene would be quickly diluted in the vastly larger gene pool of Brazilian bees. They were wrong.

The bee—*Apis mellifera adansonii*—proved biologically cunning as well as irascible. It was an invader. Settling under a beehive, African bees would enter, kill the reigning queen and replace her with their own. Soon, having reproduced to the point of crowding, some Africans would swarm and settle in the wilds. The Africans seemed to prefer trees for their hives, but they were capable of attacking an anthill, driving out the ants and remodeling the hill for themselves. As many as a hundred African hives per square mile had been counted. Because of its vitality, skill at robbing other bees of their honey stores, and most of all its genetic dominance, *adansonii* had accomplished a biological miracle. Like the Huns, it swept forward. In a single decade the twenty-six swarms and their descendants had suppressed and Africanized the whole bee population of Brazil. Almost all Brazilian bees could now be called African.

The fury of which the African was capable had been recorded near São Paulo when an African hive was discovered in a chimney and set on fire. Instantly, said a local newspaper, "a buzzing mass covered the sun." The Africans stung over five hundred people and left behind a trail of writhing or dead chickens and dogs. In widespread regions of Brazil the Africans had caused human fatalities, disrupted transportation and farming, changed the nature of beekeeping and caused great public anxiety.

And the invasion was spreading at the rate of more than two hundred miles a year. If the Africans weren't stopped they would reach the United States by the late 1970s, some thought —with results already seen in South America. But in an advanced economy such as that of the United States the situation might be disastrous. One reason was the bee's extreme sensitivity to vibrations. Here, with so much heavy equipment in use, the bee would be in a state of constant agitation.

McAllister had enclosed a map. It showed clearly the speed and range of the African penetration, halted only by the high Andes. The implications were clear.

There was talk of an antibee belt across the Central American isthmus, and other measures,* but McAllister doubted such schemes would work, even if implemented. He was convinced that the bees would invade the United States. He proposed to return to Brazil and run a full-scale study on African genetics. Most bee men believed that if the Africans did enter the United States, the temperate climate would keep them in check. McAllister worried that the Africans, which had already shown their adaptability, might produce a hybrid capable of spreading throughout the United States.

Wood was also among the scientists concerned about the Africans. He favored supporting McAllister, and said so.

Hubbard chose to balk. "I still don't believe the scare stories. They still sound fishy to me. What are the fatality figures supposed to be in Brazil?"

"About a hundred and fifty persons a year," Wood said.

"That's got to be the product of the overheated Latin imagi-

* Norman E. Gary, "Possible Approaches to Controlling the African Honey Bee," *American Bee Journal*, No. 11 (1971), Vol. III, 426–429.

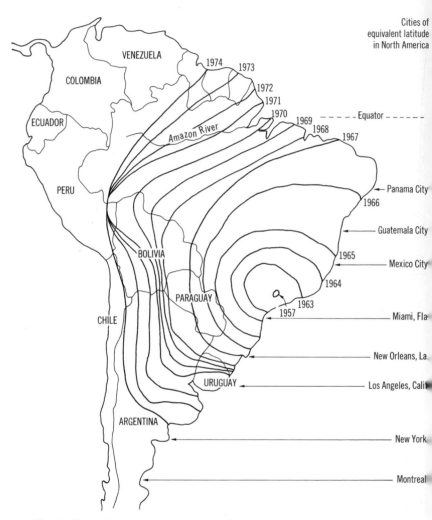

Fig. I: Distribution and spread of *adansonii* hybrid in South America. Adapted from Townsend, 1972. (Courtesy National Academy of Sciences)

nation. And too many American scientists are looking for a winter vacation in a warm climate."

Wood could almost see Hubbard's mind working. He bought a theory that even if the Africans came in American beekeepers would kill them the moment they showed in a hive. Usually it was hopeless to argue with Hubbard when he'd made up his mind, but Wood thought this issue was worth the effort. "That insect's a dangerous customer," he said in his faint drawl. "McAllister's right—we don't know nearly enough about it yet."

"What makes you so sure it won't mutate out okay?" Hubbard asked. "It's already turned peaceable in southern Brazil."

"And what makes you think it'll stay that way?" Wood asked in turn. "It's our job to worry about it."

Hubbard said stubbornly, "You worry about it. I won't. Case closed."

Wood hesitated. "Did you read about the bee killings in upstate New York?"

Hubbard's deep-set eyes stared from under upswept brows. "Yes. So what?"

"Where else have you heard about mass attacks like that?"

Hubbard grinned. "You believe they're Africans?"

"I'm just saying that's how Africans act in Brazil. Maybe a few have gotten in, yes. It's possible."

"Africans in any form would have been reported long ago. Those bees are in South America, and they won't get visas. Forget them." He was looking at Wood with a quizzical expression. "Hey, John, I think you've got a bee complex, like mine about rats. Bees frighten you, don't they?"

Thrown off guard, Wood said, "Why do you ask?"

"Look at your fingers."

Wood glanced down in surprise and saw that his fingernails were drumming an involuntary tattoo on the tabletop. He admitted he had an irrational fear of bees.

"Lots of people do, but not me," Hubbard said. "I like the

little critters. I admire their social organization and ethos. *Apis* tries harder."

The walls of Wood's office were hung with touristy color photographs of Washington attractions, like the Capitol and the cherry blossoms. They had been there when he arrived five years before, and he had never bothered to replace them.

One wall contained a large bulletin board with the names of Wood's principal projects in large printed letters.

GULF COAST SUPERPORTS

THE BIOSPHERE AND SUPERSONIC TRANSPORT AIRCRAFT

ENVIRONMENTAL IMPACT, CENTRAL CALIFORNIA WATER PROJECT

STUDY OF THE EFFECTS OF THE DALLAS-FORT WORTH REGIONAL
    AIRPORT ON DEVELOPMENT OF THE NORTH TEXAS URBAN
    COMPLEX

COMMITTEE TO DEFINE CRITERIA FOR IDENTIFYING WILDERNESS
    AREAS

Five years ago there hadn't been such projects because few people were sufficiently future-oriented then. Even people who should have known better sometimes hadn't. Even now they often acted shortsightedly. At that moment Wood was thinking of Hubbard.

John Wood was thirty-five, six feet tall, thin, with a straight nose, blue eyes, angular cheeks, an affable but controlled mouth and a military set to his shoulders. He had the sort of face women reacted to, but on the second look, not the first. He hadn't married, he told himself, because he hadn't found the right girl. Actually, he did his best to stay out of love.

Wood was from Arizona. He had gotten his Ph.D. in biology at Harvard, put in two years in the army on secret scientific research, emerging as a captain, returned to Harvard for post-doctoral work in environmental studies and become a junior fellow. He had no real liking for laboratory research, or the "bench," as scientists put it, and no real inclination to teach. The job at the National Academy was tailor-made for his aptitudes—a strong analytic mind, a good memory, a talent for diplomacy and a deep understanding of the meaning of modern technology. It had been Wood who was responsible for establishing the National Academy committee which concluded that a large fleet of supersonic transports might lower ozone levels in the upper atmosphere and expose the world to intolerable amounts of radiation.

Wood also had a flair for ideas, which, in his business, translated as an ability to anticipate trouble. He thought of this as his private Distant Early Warning System.

If Wood's personal DEW line was activated now, he had to put what Hubbard had called his "bee complex" into the equation. Wood did not regard himself as especially complicated, but he had this quirk. As a child on his father's small ranch near Tucson, he had been riding when a bee stung his horse on the nose. The horse bucked and threw Wood into a mesquite tree. Wild honeybees had attacked him savagely, stinging him on the face and both arms. But what affected him most strongly—and figured in the recurrent dreams he had had ever since—was the chase. Not content with stinging him repeatedly, the furious bees had pursued him across the desert as though to drive home a lesson he would never forget. To his ten-year-old mind, it seemed as though he had run a mile, and perhaps he had—flailing his arms, sobbing, screaming for his mother. Each time he thought the ordeal was over, the buzzing in the sky would begin again. The bees chased him all the way to the ranch house. His mother extracted the stings, bathed him in cold water and put him to bed, where he stayed for a day. Thereafter the bees came off and on again in his dreams, pursuing him as he rode across a desert. On bad nights they stung him to death.

Wood's fear of bees had not sent him running to a psychia-

35

trist. He had the dreams occasionally, and sometimes buzzing insects made him jump or even break into a clammy sweat. One day, he was sure, the bee complex would cure itself, and in the meantime it had never affected his life or career. But now the African bee question had triggered his Distant Early Warning System, and he asked himself if the bee complex could be causing him to overreact.

Wood's small, square office left little room to pace. He took a few steps to and from the window, picked up the phone and called McAllister at Lawrence, Kansas. The entomologist answered.

"Sorry. No dice, Mac," Wood said. "Hubbard won't be budged. He thinks there's a good possibility the Africans will turn out to be nice guys."

McAllister had a high-pitched voice. It sounded resigned. "Fat chance. He'll talk out of the other side of his mouth when the goddamned things cross the Rio Grande. He can't just sit around and hope for a favorable mutation."

"He wanted to know why the bee was more peaceable in southern than northern Brazil. I didn't have any real answer. The north is tropical, the south temperate—so a cooler climate calms them?"

"That's not it," McAllister said. "The bee colonies in the south are larger and stronger. They put up more of a fight. They'll succumb eventually. Those Africans are bastards, I tell you."

Wood said suddenly, "Did you hear about what happened at a place called Maryville?"

McAllister said he hadn't. When Wood explained, the apiologist whistled so loudly Wood thought there was trouble on the line. "That's exactly how our African friends behave." He paused. "But I can't see any possibility of them getting to New York State."

36

"Suppose an African were found. Could it be identified easily?"

"Maybe. There's been so much interbreeding between bees that it's hard to know one from another. In theory, *adansonii* ought to be a little smaller than American bees, but that's uncertain too. Even Bill Birch at the Smithsonian had trouble certifying the California bees as genuine Africans."

"California bees?" Wood said quickly.

"The ones that came off a ship at Richmond."

"What happened?" Wood said, feeling suddenly disturbed.

To Wood it seemed that McAllister's high-pitched voice had risen higher. "Well, in '72, at Richmond, near San Francisco, dock workers found bees in the hold of a ship. Bees can travel by ship, you know, or practically any other way. Containerized shipping is ideal for them—they build combs right in the containers. By the time the Agriculture guys got there, the bees had swarmed. They were found on a dock and gassed. The whole thing is something of a mystery, because the ship had come from Japan. It had stopped earlier in San Pedro, so maybe the bees jumped to this ship from another ship there. One ship at San Pedro had been in Guatemala, but the Africans aren't supposed to have reached Guatemala yet. The specimens were sent to Birch at the National Museum. He's tops at identifying insects, and he says they're African."

Wood said sharply, "Did they find the queen?"

McAllister seemed uncomfortable. "As a matter of fact, they didn't, no."

Wood said, "Well, the implication is that they may have gotten in, either in that instance or others."

"California's a long way from New York."

Wood tried to keep the irritation out of his voice and almost succeeded. "It might have helped if you'd told me this before I talked to Hubbard."

"There are no real facts to go on, and I didn't want to over-load my argument," McAllister piped. He sounded defensive.

Wood said, "Well, I guess it wouldn't have affected Hubbard's decision. And the possibility that the African's in is very remote."

"On the order of zero," McAllister answered.

"Still, I'd like to be sure."

3

THE BEEKEEPER

That same day Henry David was closing his books for the honey season. Columns of figures marching down his ledger told of the most spectacular summer in his forty-five years of beekeeping. The weather had been ideal for flowers—early rains, plenty of sun, not too hot or too cold—and never had he seen so many blossoms. Rising to the occasion, the bees had worked harder than any bees in his long experience, up early and out late.

On the wall of his trailer David had taped a photograph from a bee journal. It showed the Ohio Honey Queen, golden-haired and creamy-breasted, wearing a sign that read *Honey Bees Are the Angels of Agriculture*. Henry David agreed.

He had been calling himself Henry David for so long that he had almost forgotten the name on his birth certificate. Decades ago, as a quirky, shy and secretive young man, with a hatred for both government and people, he had left his wife and closeted himself in this underpopulated region of New York. There he set up as a beekeeper, determined, despite his lack of literary background, to model himself after his hero, Thoreau. He felt no regrets, no desire to end his monastic solitude. With his bees around he never felt alone.

When he wanted to talk he talked to the bees. "Hey, little girls! Hey, little fellars!"

The bees were his slaves. They worked hard but were allowed

to keep only just enough of their production to stay alive. Still they gave him no back talk. They were nice critters to have around.

Besides, bees amused him. He smiled at the thought of the eager drones hanging around in packs as they waited for the queens, as the young bucks at the ice cream parlor waited for skirts. How affectionate some bees were—they would come and sit on his arms and shoulders without fear. Two of his hives were especially gentle toward him, but not to the other bees. Toward the rest, these bees were scrappy, even violent. They kept to themselves, to the point of mating only with their own group. This was because of the habit these queens and drones had of going on their mating flights in the morning, not in the early afternoon like the other bees. That was nature's way, David thought, of not letting them propagate a bad seed, for these bees were dumb. They gathered no honey to speak of, only pollen, in huge amounts, which they hoarded. Without David to feed them they would have starved. Bees were strange!

Henry David found it charming and wonderful that a creature only a half inch long, with a brain hardly larger than a pinhead, could perform so many complex operations, such as heating a hive in winter, cooling it in summer, communicating to others the exact location of flowers it had found a mile away, locating the sun through a bank of clouds, building perfect hexagonal cells without a blueprint. Still, like all beekeepers, David struggled to improve his family, to develop bees that were big producers of honey, docile, and resistant to such diseases as American foulbrood, which could wipe out a hive.

Once a year Henry David left his bees. Many beekeepers kill off their stock in the fall and buy new bees in the spring, but David's bees were allowed to try to survive the winter, though many would die. In late February he set off in his pickup truck for the South, where the bee breeders were, and there he would buy new bees to repopulate and improve his hives. The breeders were using all means possible, including artificial insemination, to come up with ever better bee strains. Over the years David had shopped for bees all over the South, though he had come to have a preference for a large, isolated Florida apiary located in a grove of mango trees. His buying over, he gave himself his yearly reward, a trip to a seedy, small-town brothel, and headed home with the new bees, arriving in time for the first bloom of dandelions, willows and maples.

Although he was the keeper, occasionally David wondered if the bees weren't using him, instead of the other way round. Their mentality amazed him. Even bees that would never live to see winter seemed to know instinctively that summer would come again for the colony. There didn't appear to be any sense of the present with bees, as though what was happening now was really a part of next year or the year after.

That was why what looked cruel to humans about the bee world wasn't cruel from the bees' point of view. The drone who perished after he'd mated was only doing his job. And she, the queen, returning to the hive with the drone's organ sticking out of her, was like the women who used to hang out bloody sheets to prove that marriage had been consummated. Once her organ, from multiple matings, was full of enough sperm to last her whole life she became nothing more than a machine for laying two or three thousand eggs a day. That was doing her job. The others were always watching her. If she began to falter at her laying, they wouldn't sting her—the inbred respect for royalty forbade that. Instead, they chose a means of execution in which no single individual could be held responsible, like a firing squad. They balled her, clustering around her in such numbers that she was crushed or suffocated. She didn't fight to live; it was her job to die.

Bees were the exact opposite of people, David thought. People

41

seemed to have no sense of the future of their race, but cared only for themselves and their immediate wants. Bees, on the other hand, cared only for the future and nothing for themselves. Even stinging was altruistic: for a bee, to sting was to die.

Henry David understood bees—at least before this summer he had thought so. The bees had been acting strangely, and had confused, even frightened him a little, although he didn't like to admit it to himself. In one sense, at least, bees were like people: give them half a chance and they stole. You could spot a delinquent bee by its appearance. Creeping through small holes into neighboring hives to avoid detection by guards posted at the main entrance, a robber bee literally scraped the hair from its body. He had never seen so many robber bees before.

And then there was the propolis, a resinous substance bees collect from tree buds and use to keep the hive walls smooth and waterproof. Out in the wilds bees need propolis, but it is a beekeeper's nightmare. To keep a hive functioning he must scrape it off. This summer propolis production had been greater than David had ever seen it. The scraping had almost exhausted him. In one corner of his mind the suspicion had grown that the bees were finding plastic and using it in their propolis; he had found tiny grains of what looked to him like Styrofoam. It had happened before, apparently. The great naturalist Maeterlinck had reported to unbelieving bee men that *Apis* could utilize cement.

Henry David's bees had changed in other ways too—such as sound. Beyond the usual pipings and strummings, the *seep-seep* of queens waiting to mate, the trumpetlike war cry of a queen ready to do battle with another, the squeal of a hurt queen, the wail of a queenless hive, there was a particular set of bee noises David always listened for. One was *zzzzzzzzzz*, which told of contentment, the hum of a hive celebrating a good day in the fields. *Zeeeeee* said, "Attention! Stay away"—and was meant earnestly to be obeyed. Finally, at the top of the scale was *ziiiiii,* the cry of pure bee hatred. Sometimes *ziiiiii* was accompanied by an actual odor, a war smell, the smell of attack.

Henry David did not often hear *ziiiiii,* because he left the area the moment any of his bees appeared anxious. He knew that beekeepers had died from the explosive reactions of angry bees. This summer he had heard the warning note more often, and did not know why. Possibly he had got a bad strain from the breeders; with artificial insemination being used, there were greater chances for error. Perhaps he had some Germans on his hands; German bees were bad-tempered, and David tried to avoid them. Most likely, though, it was the robbings. Bee populations, like human ones, become restless and agitated when there is crime in the neighborhood.

A new note had been sounded too, which escalated almost to a roar. He had heard it only late at night, and it puzzled him, for never in his beeyard had he heard such a noise. He sometimes imagined that it was his twenty-million-member family celebrating the most bountiful summer in their history. But was that what it meant?

Finally, that summer he had lost bees. Henry David could usually forestall swarming. Even when he failed, the bees would fly to a nearby branch or fence post, and while they sent out scouts to decide what to do next, it was a simple matter to recapture them. Not these bees. No less than twenty-five swarms had absconded without warning, streaking off like arrows and not turning back. Ordinarily the loss would have mattered, but this summer, with ten tons of honey to sell, David hadn't cared. Still, he wondered what had become of them. Perhaps they were the property of another beekeeper by now, perhaps because a bee hunter had captured them—he hoped so. Most probably, however, they were holed up in a hollow tree somewhere, hungry and despondent, having taken with them only six days' honey supply. An old adage crossed his mind:

A swarm of bees in May is worth a ton of hay.
A swarm of bees in June is worth a silver spoon.
A swarm of bees in July ain't worth a fly.

Bees that absconded in late July, as his had, didn't have time to prepare for winter. They would die.

Henry David could feel winter in the air, and there was work to do. He had about four hundred colonies, each in its own hive. Each had to be checked out, and a sugar solution given those that had an insufficient honey supply for winter. At the first hive a bee stung David on the hand. Preoccupied, he had been moving faster than he ought. Henry David didn't really mind. Bee stings, he felt sure, were the reason he hadn't a trace of arthritis or rheumatism although he was close to seventy. Carefully, he removed the sting. Left in, it would continue to pump poison ever deeper into the flesh. Long immune to bee venom, his flesh would not swell. But no matter how often you had been stung, it always hurt.

4

THE ENTOMOLOGICAL ASSOCIATION

The annual meeting of the American Entomological Association, held this year in New York, attracted about two thousand scientists from many disciplines. From Wednesday through Saturday at the Hilton Hotel they would sit on folding chairs, listen to papers, exchange ideas, attend cocktail parties and look for jobs, funding and sport. It was a convention like any other.

Looking over the thick printed program, John Wood was struck by the tenor of the proceedings. The tone seemed almost military—like that of a council of war. There was continual emphasis on the offensive-defensive quality of the struggle between the insect world and human beings. For the first time science was peering deeply into the sociobiology of insects, and the findings were not reassuring. The insects had evolved sophisticated systems of communications, organization and control that seemed, more and more, to parallel those developed by human beings. Nor were insects so locked into hereditary patterns as had been thought. Many insects appeared to be startlingly flexible, and changing rapidly.

This was the point raised by Robert Gerston, Ph.D., Columbia University, at a panel session the first afternoon. Gerston was an old friend of Wood's from Harvard. A vanishing kind, Gerston did entomology in the field when most other entomologists were studying biology in a lab. He was a six-foot-four, rawboned man with a battering ram of a nose. Recently he had concluded a field trip to South Vietnam, where he had collected a large number of grasshoppers. Cornell scientists had reported tentatively that the grasshopper *Romales microptera* was able to secrete a froth that contained a chlorinated compound. Since these compounds were almost absent in nature, the scientists deduced that the grasshoppers were absorbing it and using it as a defense weapon, probably against ants, which would be repelled by the odor. If true, this marked the first known case where an insect had succeeded in using a man-made substance for its own defense.*

Gerston proved that South Vietnamese grasshoppers were using chemicals absorbed from defoliants, and not just in their foam but in their excreta as well, which could evidently be released in times of danger.

When the questions were over, Wood beckoned to Gerston with his finger. Gerston followed him into the hall, where they sat down. They chatted a moment about Gerston's new baby, and then Wood drawled softly, "I had a call from the science editor of the *Times*. He wanted to know if your findings were accurate."

Gerston frowned. "I wish they weren't."

"I told him they were, though. You said on the phone there was something else."

Gerston peered down the hall. Then he said, "Well, in a way there is. I mean, it's not the sort of thing you necessarily want to commit to paper. Once you've written it, you sound as though you believe it, no matter how you hedge. Know what I mean?"

Wood said he did.

Gerston uncrossed his long legs. "You understand how the study was conducted? We caught a large number of grasshoppers and brought them back. The secretion was obtained by gently squeezing individuals and collecting the froth and the excreta. What we got was a few drops of fluid, which were

* *Science*, 172:277 (April 1971).

carefully analyzed. The herbicides showed up clearly. That wasn't all." He paused.

Wood said, "Go on."

"Well, in addition to the defoliant compounds there was DDT. I don't mean merely an unassimilated residue—there has to be some of that, because the Vietnamese use the stuff. This DDT was combined with the grasshoppers' defensive substances, just as the herbicides were. The quantity was minute, and I'm not prepared to publish anything without more research. But there is now evidence that 'hoppers have learned to use insecticides for defense. I thought I'd let you know."

Wood's angular face wrinkled in concentration. He said slowly, "The implications are staggering."

"It's a little like equipping the insect world not just with conventional weapons but with atomic bombs to use against each other. I just can't imagine the results for them."

Wood said the obvious. "Or for us."

At scientific conferences like these Wood always floated, drifting from panel to panel, listening to the arguments. In one, there was a spirited discussion in progress. An entomologist argued that the small size of insects was their greatest evolutionary asset. It enabled them to survive every catastrophe. Another accused him of being old-fashioned. Recent electron-microscope studies of ant brains revealed them to be complex mechanisms with extraordinary refinements in brain tissues that could be compared only to the most complex human electronics. Insects, this entomologist said, are smarter than we think.

A brilliant young geneticist, Walter Krim, got up to argue that long-term adaptation by man to permit him to compete successfully for scarce resources might require that he become smaller, perhaps half his present size. Wood admired the man's temerity. Krim, he judged, was only five-foot-five.

Wood stopped at the doorway to one conference room, not

because of what he heard but because of what he saw. A lithe, dark-haired young woman was presenting statistics on what she claimed were increased deaths among California farm workers. She had barely finished when the scientists began to attack her arguments, driving her close to tears. It was her figure, not figures, that had got to them, Wood thought, smiling, and moved on.

He saw her again that evening at the cocktail party held to kick off the conference. She stood by herself, collected, but looking nowhere in particular, in a room overwhelmingly male. Perhaps it was her guarded expression that put the scientists off, or perhaps it was her looks that made them shy. She was exceptionally attractive. Tall and slim, she had flat, almost Indian cheeks, olive skin, long, narrow eyes, a butterfly mouth, and a high forehead with thick black hair pulled above it. Give the scientists a few drinks and they'd be all over her, Wood thought.

Wood was debating whether to approach her when he discovered that his feet had settled the argument for him. He put his hand out and said his name. Her badge read, "Maria Amaral, M.D., College of Agriculture and Environmental Sciences, University of California, Davis."

Wood said that he'd heard the entomologists attack her paper. They'd acted like louts, he told her.

Dr. Amaral raised her head quickly. The eyes behind large gold-framed glasses were solemn, watchful and black. Wood felt as though he had been struck physically in the face. "Are all American men clouts?" she asked.

"Louts," he said. "You're not American?"

"I'm Brazilian."

For Wood, at that exact moment things began to operate on two levels that seemed to have no relation to each other. She told him about herself, and he listened, but all the while he was thinking of a word he rarely used—"pheromone," or chemical messenger. He was aware of something being transmitted between them. He was certain, too, that it wasn't visual or related to anything being said. Clearly it was affecting her too. Her eyes had become hot and shiny, as though they were covered with a light film. The mysterious messenger seemed to pass back and forth, laying a trail between them.

Maria Amaral was a medical doctor with a degree in epidemiology from an American university, which accounted for her mastery of English. In Brazil she was a public-health official for her government, studying long-range disease patterns. She was twenty-eight, single, and, Wood guessed, single-minded about her work.

Her government had sent her to Davis for a year to study the training of farm workers in the use of organophosphate pesticides. These pesticides had all but replaced DDT, but although they were a lesser hazard to the environment than DDT, they could be dangerous to farm workers if handled improperly. As the United States had already done, Brazil was switching to organophosphates, but there were many backward farmers in Brazil whose lives would be in jeopardy if they didn't understand how carefully organophosphates must be handled.

Dr. Amaral explained that she had concentrated her effort in Yolo County, California. She spoke, in addition to Portuguese and English, perfect Spanish, and she talked with the farm workers, most of whom were Chicanos. There were many stories of sickness and death, she said—too many.

It was not part of her job, but instinct had brought her to the county medical seat. She asked to see the death records of Chicano farm workers, and was refused—why, she did not know. She guessed because she was a woman, because they took her for Chicano, because the bureaucrats didn't want anyone looking over their shoulders, or any or all of these reasons. No study such as the one she intended was needed, they said. They did not propose to admit her to the room where the death records were kept.

Maria, eyes blazing like tropical moons, had pulled herself to her full five-foot-seven and said, "I am *Doctor* Maria Teresa de Moura Amaral, and I *demand* to inspect those records *now*."

As she related this in the crowded ballroom, even re-creating the expression she had used, Wood could imagine the impact she must have had on the county medical officials. Inevitably, they relented. What followed was not so amusing. Amaral made a detailed actuarial study of farm-worker deaths, inspecting each certificate. To decide which individuals had been farm workers, she used the only test available—she made the assumption that all the male deceased with such Spanish names as Rodriguez or Vargas were farm workers. She learned that their death rate had been higher than that for the general population for the past three years, and that it was increasing. To a professional medical statistician like herself this clustering of deaths in one occupational group had to have a reason.

The jump in the death rate appeared to have been caused by heart attacks. But Amaral knew that there was a strong superficial resemblance between organophosphate poisoning and certain kinds of heart attacks. She knew, too, that coroners' handling of deaths tended to be routine, especially Chicano deaths. A man found dead in the sun would be put down as a heart-attack victim without an autopsy or even an analysis of his blood.

The county medical people had smiled at her. They doubted statistics that assumed everyone with a Spanish name to be a farm worker. Nor did Maria's colleagues at Davis pay attention to her, a foreigner who was there for only a year. Paying her own fare, she had come to the Entomological Association to get a hearing. And once again she had been ignored.

She may be excitable, but she's thorough, she's persistent, Wood thought. "People dislike uncertainty. They insist on answers, even if they are pat answers or the wrong answers," he said to her. He suggested that she interview the families of the deceased. If she could find a good reason to doubt the coroner in a number of cases, she would have a basis for challenging the county's version of the facts. Maria said she would try.

John listened, but he was more absorbed by Maria than by what she was saying. Later he wondered if he would have been more guarded if she had not been scheduled to return to California so soon, on Sunday. But there was no need to talk about it.

He could not remember afterward exactly what of a personal nature had been said—very little, he felt sure—or when the decision had been made. But it had been made—quickly, naturally, mutually, with the innocence provided by inevitability.

A friend, in Europe on a sabbatical, had given Wood the use of a West Side apartment, and there they went. Of Wood's experience that night he told no one, not even Maria Amaral. He kissed her brow, cheeks, neck, burying his lips in skin the color of light rum, in hair the texture of boll cotton. Approaching, entering her, he had the sensation that he flew, ever higher, drawn inescapably by his queen.

Friday evening Wood suggested that they skip the last (always boring) session of the conference, rent a car and take a drive. Maria could see a little of the Eastern countryside. Wood said vaguely that there was something he wanted to do.

The West Side apartment had a terrace that overlooked Central Park. The endless summer was over; Wood's arm around her, Maria shivered under her wrap. Pressing her face against his cheek, she said, "I want to sniff your pheromoons."

"Pheromones," he said, laughing.

"How do they work?"

"Insects secrete them. There's a moth whose pheromones can attract a mate from more than six miles away. It's as if you were in Brazil and I were in Washington. Imagine detection and following particles in that sea of air."

"What happens when the pheromones wear off?" she said lightly. "Are the insects still attracted?"

"I doubt it. But human beings aren't insects," he said. "I hope."

John Wood had never been happier. Something about this woman pulled him out of his usual preoccupations and made him light-headed, free. But staring from the terrace, he felt a chill that had nothing to do with fall. North gleamed the lights of Harlem, like lace on black. Across the park the East Side loomed like a fairy citadel. South were the Essex House, the Plaza Hotel, the RCA Building—symbols of American power and wealth, most prominent of which was the General Motors Building, white marble front rising in a sheer plane toward the dark sky. New York, for all its flaws, had to be regarded as a monument, the way the pyramids must have seemed to the ancient world. He wondered if New York would stand as long as the pyramids had stood. There was no reason why not, and yet tonight he had a foreboding that the city was vulnerable.

That night, after they made love, he had another dream. Angry bees chased him across an endless Dali desert, tormenting him, scorching him, until, wounded and dying, he fell. Towering over all was an enormous compound eye—the eye of an insect—on a stalk. In terror, moaning and sweating, he put his face into Maria's bare shoulder and smelled her skin, which seemed to calm him even in his sleep.

5

MARYVILLE

Anxious to preserve the mood of their brief idyll, John Wood had put off telling Maria about the bees in Maryville. Now, on the Taconic Parkway in a rented car, he did. She was from Brazil and might know something about the Africans.

Maria Amaral took a short breath. "In Brazil the apiaries have been moved far from the cities. Some have barbed-wire fences and signs that say 'Danger—Keep Out.' The beekeepers can work the hive only at night, the bees are so vicious. The government passed a rule that African bees were to be exterminated, but rescinded it when they realized that meant all the bees. They are still trying to introduce European bees into the hives to crossbreed, but so far they haven't succeeded. The African drones are too fast and too strong for the European ones, I believe. I remember a terrible day when I was in school. It was a country schoolhouse on my father's estates. The bees attacked on the playground and we ran inside. They kept us holed up for two hours there. You could hear them banging against the door and windows as they tried to get in." She shuddered. "Finally they left."

"Let's hope they're right—that there's no chance the Africans have come here," John said. Maria said that she seemed to remember hearing a good deal of talk about bees behaving strangely on the West Coast. John's lean face showed nothing, but his fingers drummed on the steering wheel.

Just as Maria had done in California, John was now pursuing an investigation that was outside the normal limits of his job. But Wood wanted to rule out any chance that the bees that had attacked near Maryville were Africans. Whatever they were, those bees were still at large.

Maryville. Pop. 2,073 a small sign announced. John's ecological eye noted an open garbage dump. He also saw second-growth timber, which indicated farming had ceased in these parts. He mentally classified the area as economically depressed. Only a few blocks long, the main street of Maryville had the usual assortment—a movie house, a few bars, some rooming houses, a bowling alley, an antique store that probably had bargains, a laundromat, a five-and-dime, a drugstore. There was a handsome ice cream parlor with a plate-glass window and a white gingerbread front, which looked as though it were the center of Maryville's social life.

Wood parked the car, pausing to admire a lovely old tree in the town square. He went into the ice cream parlor to find a phone. Teen-age kids crowded noisily in booths. Wood had brought the newspaper clipping from Washington. He looked up David P. Znac in the phone book.

Dr. David P. Znac would be happy to see them in his office down the street. When Wood opened the door a buzzer sounded in the back of the house. They entered a reception room paneled in what John called, in a low voice, "snotty pine." There was a desk but no receptionist. He decided Znac was the sort of doctor who waited around Saturday afternoons for whatever business happened to come along. It wouldn't be much.

A TV set was turned off, and Znac emerged in his shirt sleeves, a middle-aged man with a pencil-size mustache. The butt of a small revolver protruded from his belt. John introduced Maria, and Znac examined her with obvious admiration. He led them to his office, and Wood, after they had sat down, repeated what he had said on the phone. He looked at Znac's revolver and said, "Any special reason for that?"

Znac said with quick bitterness, "Six months ago fellow down the road, a veterinarian, was held up in his office—teen-age thugs, we think—and shot to death. Never caught them, though."

"You wouldn't expect violent crime around here," Wood observed.

"It didn't use to happen before," Znac said. "But now it does. Can't blame drugs, either. We don't have a real problem like that. It's something deeper—some weakening of the prohibition against taking a human life. But I'm a doctor, not a philosopher. What can I tell you about the Petersons? They were a nice young couple. He worked at the lumberyard."

"In my line we're always keeping an eye out for mutations, good and bad," Wood said. "If a strain of exceptionally aggressive insect developed, we'd want to know about it. The attack by bees last Sunday seemed strange to me. There are not that many wild bees anymore."

"Strange, maybe, but not for that reason," Znac answered. He took a homemade cigarette from a case and lit it. "Lots of folks forget that Mother Nature goes right on out there without us. I'm willing to bet there are as many wild bees in these parts as there are in beeyards. These woods are perfect for them. Ask any bee hunter."

"Bee hunter?" Wood asked.

Under the mustache Znac's gray teeth mocked the scientist for being a city yokel. "It's a sport. I do it myself. You find a hive in the woods and claim the honey. A wild colony attacked the Petersons. The nearest beeyard, old man David's, is ten miles from the place."

"But bees don't normally attack like that," Wood said.

"Normal?" Znac glanced at his watch, evidently decided it

was time, reached into his desk, pulled out a bottle of bourbon and paper cups, and glanced at Maria, who, to John's surprise, nodded. He poured a splash in each cup. "I've never heard of it happening, but it happened. Maybe a bear—though, really, I doubt that. Not many bears hereabouts anymore. Tree came down, more likely. Bees build in hollow trees that are alive, but maybe this hive made a mistake and picked a dead one. Or maybe the tree was weakened by the windstorm we had here a little while ago. There they were, no home for winter, no time to make another, and feeling desperate and mean. So they were resting in a hollow log, and the kid comes along and kicks it. Out they come, fighting mad. I wouldn't call it normal exactly, but there has to be some explanation."

The doctor's doubts about his own theory showed. But, Wood thought, as Znac had said, what's normal? "The cause of death in both cases was a fatal allergic reaction?"

Znac nodded slowly. "That's about right. Certainly true of the husband. He took only about a dozen stings. Typical anaphylactic symptomatology."

John looked at Maria, who added, "Fourth-degree anaphylaxis. A reaction incompatible with life. Laryngeal edema— swelling of the larynx. Cardiovascular reaction—heart stops. Perhaps lesions in the nervous system."

"I warned him," Znac went on, giving Maria a glance that was half respectful and half leering. "He got stung by a wasp ten years ago and swelled up pretty bad. I told him he ought to get desensitized." He shrugged.

"What about the woman?"

"That's harder. Mary took maybe a hundred hits. As few as fifty can be fatal. She saved the kids in a way—the bees concentrated on her. She looked like she'd been worked over by a cactus. Stings all over, even in her mouth. Cause of death was definitely the venom in her bloodstream. But I'd be willing to bet she had an allergic shock reaction, which was why she couldn't run away. So anaphylaxis can be considered the cause of death here too."

Wood had decided that Znac wasn't a bad sort, but he suffered from a problem—drinking, maybe. "You seem to know your stuff, Dr. Znac," he said.

"Try to. Too many coroners don't. Most of them aren't even doctors. I bet a lot more people die from bee stings than are reported. They're put down as heart attacks. Even doctors can make mistakes. A bee sting could be under the hair and not seen. The doctor thinks it's a heart attack and gives digitalis. It's wrong. Curtains."

Dr. Amaral looked up sharply.

"How are the kids?" Wood asked.

"The boys are okay. Tim swam across the stream and Randy ran to the road, where Himmel, the garbage man, found him." He laughed. "They have a lot of crazy stories."

"Stories?" Wood said.

"That those bees were as big as golf balls, that the bees ate plastic, that the whole sky was black with bees. It must have been pretty awful. I don't blame them for exaggerating."

"And the girl?"

"She's still laid up. She got it worse than the boys, and you sometimes have complicated neurological aftereffects from something like this. She'll be all right." It seemed to Wood that a flicker of anxiety crossed Znac's face.

"I'd like to talk to them."

"I don't know what they can tell you, but I don't see any reason why not."

They finished the drinks in the paper cups. At the office door John stopped. "Where do you think those bees are now?"

Znac crossed the room and looked at a thermometer in the window. "It's about fifty. The hive will be huddled in a ball trying to keep warm. They don't have food. They won't hurt anybody now. When it drops a few degrees they'll die."

The waiting room was still empty. As they passed out the front door they could hear the sudden roar of Znac's TV.

The small clapboard house was two blocks away. The kids were staying with Mary Peterson's older, widowed sister. Thelma Billings appeared to be a woman accustomed to sorrow. She seemed constantly on the verge of wringing her hands.

"Terrible, awful," she said to them. "Those poor kids. The funeral expenses. Oh Jesus." She didn't bother to ask the reason for the visit, as though too numb to care.

John Wood waited with Maria Amaral in the living room while the woman fetched the boys from the backyard. It was a dark room filled with bric-a-brac. Past the hallway an open doorway led to what looked to be a bedroom with drawn blinds, where, he guessed, Karen lay in bed.

Both boys had reddish welts on their faces and marks on their arms that would have passed for bruises, but they appeared normal otherwise, if subdued. When they were seated on the mohair couch, Wood said, "Boys, try to tell me about last Sunday."

The boys told how the family had gone on a picnic, how Karen caught a bee in a honey jar, how Randy dropped the jar on the log, how some bees came, how more bees came, how Karen got one stuck in her hair which stung her, how Mommy was running to help, how Mommy and Dad were dead now.

"You poor children," Maria said.

"What were the bees like?" John asked. Maria glared at him, but he persisted.

"They were big," Tim said. He made as large a circle as he could with the thumb and forefinger of one hand.

"Not *that* big."

"Oh, yes, they was," Randy cried. "Like marshmallows. Bigger even."

"And loud. Like a waterfall," Tim insisted. "They rushed

around like they was crazy. They made funny bunches, like grapes."

"They flew into the fire," Randy said.

John smiled. "Bees don't fly into fires."

"But they did! And they burned up!" Randy shouted. He looked at his brother for confirmation.

Tim nodded solemnly. "And what they ate. Cookies, cake, ice cream."

"Even hamburgers," Randy added.

"He doesn't mean hamburgers," Tim said condescendingly. "But I saw them eat plastic cups."

"Bees don't eat plastic, Tim," John said softly.

A small voice behind them said, "These ones did."

The scientists whirled. Maria said, "Oh my God."

Wearing boy's pajamas, Karen stood behind them, propping herself against the doorframe. Her face was ashen gray, her eyes half shut. Dark-red lines etched her swollen cheeks. Her lips were puffed. One of her arms was swollen to the size of an adult's. Maria went quickly to her, drawing her close. "Are you all right, child?" she asked.

"I'm dizzy and my stomach hurts." It seemed to Wood that Karen wheezed. "I itch inside."

"She vomits once in a while and she walks funny," Thelma Billings said worriedly.

Maria took a few steps back. "Walk to me, dear."

Karen started toward her, with effort. "We ate too many sweets and didn't take our vitamins," she said in a small, high, singsong voice. "That's why the bees punished us. Those awful bees! My poor Mommy was trying to come to me, but the bees, the bees . . ." She started to sob.

Maria hugged her close. Tears rose in her eyes. "Sweet little darling." She stared at John. "Karen, come in the bedroom. I want a look at you."

"I know how you feel," John said to the boys. He explained

59

how bees had chased and stung him when he was ten. "But you mustn't be scared of bees for the rest of your life, or—" He started to say, but didn't, "you'll have bad dreams."

Randy had started to wail. "I wish Mommy was back," he said, half to himself. Tim said nothing, but his upper lip quivered. Wood sat down on the couch between them with his arms around their shoulders.

Maria came out, shaking her head. "She's had a severe reaction, no doubt about that. Probably she still has a small amount of venom in her system. Beyond that . . ." She trailed off.

"Is there any danger?" Wood asked.

"I don't think so, but still I wonder if she should be checked out at the hospital."

"Znac said she'd be okay. He seems to understand bee stings."

"Yes," Maria said, "he seems to. Still, I wish I knew more about bee-sting reactions."

Both had misgivings when they left. At the door, Wood asked Thelma Billings where to find the picnic site.

Wood insisted that Maria wait for him at the antique store. If there was trouble, he said, he could get out faster alone. Protesting, she accepted his decision. But his real reason was that he did not want her to see his fear.

Warily he worked his way through the woods, turning his head this way and that. The bee chase of his childhood was so vivid in his mind that he could hear the buzz in his ears. At one point, no longer certain whether the whine of the bees was in his head or real, he was tempted to return to the car, and had to steel himself to continue. The clearing hummed faintly, but there was no sign of bees.

All at once he heard a noise that seemed both near and far away. It sounded like the shrill buzz of a tiny machine. He searched the clearing and the bushes, but the noise grew fainter, now louder, eluding him, until at last it faded altogether. A cricket, maybe.

He wanted a dead bee. More than a hundred of them must have fallen in the area after leaving their lances in the bodies of the Petersons. Wood searched carefully around the bushes and was prowling the area around the log when he saw a dirty boot by his hand.

Wood rose, feeling absurd. The boot belonged to a man with long greasy hair and a pepper-and-salt stubble. He wore a derelict combination of old clothes and carried a fishing pole. Even in the open air Wood could smell the alcohol from four feet away. "Need a hand, mister?" the man said suspiciously.

Wood decided to be straightforward, and explained that he was a scientist and looking for specimens of the bees that had attacked a family here.

The man took his remarks in stride. "Never find 'em," he announced. "Birds eat 'em. So do ants, skunks, and I don't know what all."

"Live around here?" Wood asked.

"Do, as a matter of fact. It was me who found little Randy."

"Ah, you're Mr. Himmel, then."

"Am. Tend the town dump, couple of miles from here. Got to go close up pretty soon."

"Did you see the bees that attacked the Petersons?" Wood asked.

"Nope."

Wood tried again. "Did you hear them?"

"Nope." He paused. "Too far away."

"Where did they come from, do you think?"

"Escaped from a beeyard, maybe. There are some around here, though pretty far away. Could be wild too."

"Are there a lot of bees in the woods?"

"Sure. Why not?"

This line of questioning was getting nowhere. John started to leave, then said quickly, "How's life at the dump, Mr. Himmel?"

"Oh, same. Always tell people the same thing—papers and plastic to the right, food garbage to the left, metal over by the hill. Every week I burn the stuff. Once a year we bulldoze it under. I find a nice bottle sometimes, or a good pair of boots"— he glanced at his own—"and for kicks sometimes I shoot rats."

Wood saw it all too well. This was the kind of untreated garbage dump the Environmental Protection Agency was trying to legislate out of existence. "Have a lot of bees?" he asked.

Himmel scratched the stubble on his cheek with a grimy fingernail. "Yes, I guess so. More this summer than last, come to think of it. Stay away from 'em myself."

"Anything different about them?"

The finger was probing his ear now. "Nope. Well . . . only that they're always into that damn plastic."

Not fifty yards away, high in a hollow spruce, a few large bees stood quietly at a narrow hole. The aperture of the hole had been reduced by the addition of two horizontal pillars that would serve to keep small animals out. The bees had built these pillars. In the setting sun they gleamed yellow-white, with a touch of blue.

The hollow inside the tree had been lined with the same material, so smooth that it looked as though it had been polished. It filled every chink and covered every rough spot. Waterproof and windproof, it was ideal insulation.

The bees had worked fast, taking advantage of the exceptionally good weather that had saved them. Hanging from the top of the hollow and secured at the bottom were combs six feet long, packed with honey, hundreds of pounds of it. Upon this comb, buzzing faintly, massed a hundred thousand bees.

A chill evening breeze stirred the forest. The last guard bee at the entrance hole went in. The bees on the comb moved closer together, into a ball, and the ones on the outside began gently to fan their wings for the proper circulation of heat from the massed bodies of the bees. The bee furnace had been ignited. The hive was ready for winter.

John took Maria to Kennedy Airport in a cab. She was returning to California and then to Brazil for the Christmas holidays; he was trapped in Washington—and that was that. "We'll find each other," he said.

"Like the moths," said Maria, kissing him.

6

THE MIMIC

There were, that fall, portents of the African crisis. Understandably, no significance was attached to any of them, no relationship perceived.

Bees bounced against windows.

A bee swarm was seen high over a town.

In a mountain cabin a bee swarm flew down the chimney and out an open window without making a sound.

A racehorse was stung to death by bees.

A bee swarm entered a parked car and flew off again, petrifying the driver. . . .

In the city of New York a public-relations man named Perry Goodall kept bees for a hobby in his town house on the East Side. The bees lived in a glass hive fastened to the bare brick wall of the living room, which opened onto the backyard.

Other bees lived in Manhattan, Goodall knew, in abandoned buildings, holes in walls, hollow spaces between roofs and ceilings. But he was the only real beekeeper in Manhattan. The Museum of Natural History had had a beehive once, but had gotten rid of it to avoid liability for bee stings. Goodall had laughed when he heard of this. His bees had never stung, would never sting. They harmed no one, not himself, his wife, his children or his guests, whom Goodall liked to frighten by covering his face with bees like a beard.

In winter Goodall fed the bees a sugar solution, but the rest of the year they foraged in his backyard, those of the neighbors, and probably in Central Park. One afternoon in early October Goodall got a call from his wife. She'd heard on the radio that a bee swarm was festooned on a traffic signal at Broadway and Seventy-second Street, with *Walk* and *Don't Walk* blinking underneath it. Crowds and TV crews had assembled—Manhattan, it appeared, had never seen a bee swarm before.

They were Goodall's bees, all right, he learned that evening. But by the time he got there the bees had been collected by a Brooklyn beekeeper summoned by the police. Custom has it that stray bees are the property of the finder, like salvage.

The loss of half his bees didn't matter. Goodall had a house in Connecticut where he kept more. In the spring he would replace the ones that had eloped. Still, he wondered why his little pals had abandoned him. Perhaps the beehive was too small for them, but it seemed ungrateful of the bees.

Others lost more than bees.

Outside Palo Alto a Japanese truck gardener had been spreading fertilizer on rows of winter vegetables. He was found lying face down in a furrow. The symptoms—contracted pupils, tearing, blue skin, papilledema, loss of sphincter control—indicated organophosphate poisoning, which confused the coroner; he said to himself, "The Japs know how to handle pesticides."

There was road work in Utah, which calls itself the Beehive State. A man waved a checked flag, perspiring furiously under his yellow hard hat. Behind him a rumbling bulldozer cleared a section of cracked tarmac for new pavement. A car was coming—the driver didn't even slow down.

The flagman waved harder and got ready to jump. At the last second the car veered, skidded and came to a halt on the other side of the road. The flagman opened his mouth to yell, clutched his hand and his chest, and collapsed on the rubble. He was charted DOA—dead on arrival; cause of death, heart failure.

No one noticed the welt on his finger.

Indian summer in Delaware. An excitable businessman, convinced the car he had been sold was a lemon, argued with the dealer in the lot. Suddenly he clapped his hand to his neck as if he had been shot, took a few steps, and collapsed on the hood of his automobile. The dealer took him at once to a nearby hospital, where he was treated with digitalis for heart failure. He did not respond.

These and other serious incidents came to light when, later, the bodies of those who had died from certain causes in recent months began to be exhumed.

John Wood returned to Washington as uncertain as he had been of anything in his professional life. Every instinct told him that something was wrong—his Distant Early Warning System was sounding a full alarm—and yet he had only a few clues and no hard evidence to go on.

Also, the bee dreams were happening more frequently all the time. Should they be taken as proof that his subconscious mind had succeeded in reaching conclusions his logic wouldn't accept? Or that Maryville had merely poured fuel on fears he already had?

Wood decided to talk to William Birch about the African honeybee.

Chairman of the Department of Entomology at the National Museum of Natural History, the Smithsonian Institution, Bill

Birch was no mere entomologist. Perhaps the only term comprehensive enough to describe him was one seldom used in an age of scientific specialization—"naturalist." His books and articles reached a large audience of interested laymen as well as scientists. Written in a mannered, almost courtly style, they served as reminders that there had been a day when scientists pictured nature whole instead of in fractured pieces.

In semiretirement now, Birch came to the museum Tuesdays, Thursdays and Saturdays. On a Thursday a few weeks after the visit to Maryville, Wood arrived at Birch's office. It was jammed with metal cabinets, boxes and books piled on tables. There was equipment of various sorts.

Birch himself did not seem to square with the chaos surrounding him. He was a trim man of medium height wearing a well-tailored business suit. Light-colored tortoiseshell glasses hung from a black cord around his neck. The moment Wood heard him speak, he knew that Birch was from the South.

Wood asked Birch if there was any doubt about the origin of the bees that had been sent from California. Birch shook his head. The specimens had arrived in bad condition, he said, and identification of bee races was always chancy. "There are twenty thousand species of bees, you know. We have seventy percent of them here." He gestured toward metal cabinets, which also lined the hall outside. "I'm reasonably convinced by the wings and hind legs that those bees were African. And, of course, they had to come."

"*Had* to?" Wood said, a little surprised.

"Oh, yes. For two reasons. One is that it would be so absurdly easy for the Africans to get in that it would seem strange if they didn't. Bees travel on almost anything, you know."

"And the second?"

"The nature of the beast. Have you asked yourself how an insect could be so genetically dominant that it conquered half a continent in less than a decade?"

67

Wood nodded. "I've asked myself that. Without getting a clear answer."

"Honeybees and man both originated in eastern Africa, and at about the same time, so the latest theory says," Birch began, "which might make *adansonii* the primary race from which bees sprang. Nobody knows how long this bee has been aggressive. Some say only recently, some say from the beginning. I take the latter view, I admit. In any case, where we see viciousness the bee 'sees' survival. The African bee believes its survival depends on its being nasty, particularly to its three major enemies."

Birch held up three fingers, pulling the first like a lever. Then he startled Wood. Raising his head, the distinguished scientist made a noise that sounded like *cac—cac—cac*. Birch grinned. "I'm not in good voice today. That is the cry, or is meant to be, of *Indicator indicator*, the African honey guide. She likes beeswax, but unable to get into the hive alone, she summons an ally, the honey badger, to help her. He follows her cries and signals." Birch lowered the second finger. "This badger has a patch of skin on its back about six inches in diameter. Once the bird has led him to the hive he smears musk on this patch, and the damnfool bees attack him where the musk is, which is his armor plate. So he enters the hive and steals the honey. Honey gone, the bees leave too, usually to perish. That leaves the wax for the bird."

"And the third?" Wood asked, knowing the answer.

"Man, of course. He follows the honey guide, too. When the African native found a hive he smoked it heavily and robbed it of all its honey and brood. He even used the hive for beer. Every distinct characteristic of the African bee is based on survival mechanisms against these three enemies, especially man. Only the toughest, meanest, most irascible bees had a chance to survive."

Wood took in all this. "But what has the nature of the bee got to do with its possible spread to North America?"

"Don't you see? Look—this insect is expansionary, like man himself. For it, staying in a small area would be like being in prison. It sees its survival in terms of occupying ever larger areas. If it gets wiped out in one place, it will still exist in another. Don't forget the fundamental law of biology: *Survive*." Birch paused. "As I said," he added suddenly, his southern accent sounding strongly in his words, "I've a fundamentalist streak. Maybe it's my old Southern Methodist background—I don't know. Forgive me, but are you by chance acquainted with the fine passage from Isaiah? I know it by heart. 'And it shall come to pass in that day, that the Lord shall hiss for the fly that is in the uttermost parts of the rivers of Egypt, and for the bee that is in the land of Assyria.' Wonderful word, isn't it, 'hiss'? What do you think the line means?"

Having thought a moment, Wood said, "Well, I'm no biblical scholar, but I guess flies and bees refer to armies that the Lord would summon to punish the Israelites."

"Except I'm not sure that's the whole answer. Those metaphors of antiquity usually have a factual basis. What I mean is, why should the Lord hiss for flies and bees? Why not snakes and tigers? As metaphors they would seem more appropriate. Now, one can see why flies could be associated with disease and be deemed unpleasant. Of course the flies might have been bees, in fact. But why bees themselves? Nice little *Apis mellifera*, the honey bearer? I can think of only one answer. There was a time when the honeybee was an enemy of man. That streak has been bred out of European bees. The Africans still have it."

John Wood sat for a long moment in silence. "In other words, in dominating other bees, the Africans cause them to return to an old heritage."

"Right. And what is that heritage?" Birch looked at that moment exactly like a preacher Wood had seen in a TV series on revivalist meetings. "There's no exact scientific word for it, no concept. But what it amounts to is vengeance."

•   •   •

That same day, Maria Teresa de Moura Amaral called from California. They had spoken on the telephone since parting at the airport, but this time her voice was different—hurried, tense. He thought for an instant that this must be her normal professional tone. "I've followed your advice. I didn't want to tell you until I completed the study. I interviewed the families of ten farm workers who were supposed to have died of heart attacks since 1969. I asked many questions about the month preceding the demise. At first I thought I had nothing, there wasn't a clue. Then—I don't know—one night after you had called, I reread the notes one last time. For some reason I thought of something Dr. What's-his-name—Znac—said, and there it was, plain as day. Are you there?"

"I'm here."

"In three out of ten cases death had been preceded by a bee sting within the month. Thinking that this wasn't enough, I went back and reinterviewed the other families. Memory was often hazy, but there seemed good indication that in at least six of the ten cases a bee sting had occurred within a month of death."

"You mean a single bee sting or a couple—not a mass attack?"

"That's what they said, yes. One or a few."

What a lucky break, he thought, that a person who spoke Spanish had undertaken this investigation. "Is it usual for farm workers to be stung by bees?"

"I asked about that. It is not usual, but it is not unusual either. It seems to be more usual lately than it had been before. The workers are becoming frightened of the bees. Quite a few have gotten sick for reasons they don't understand, and they associate their illness with bee stings. But I haven't told you everything."

He waited.

"I also interviewed a few families of those said to have died from organophosphate poisoning. About the same percentage of the deceased had been stung by bees too. Can you make any sense of it?"

"No. Would you write this up for me, Maria?"

"Yes—but nobody will believe me, any more than they believed me before."

"I will. Show it only to me. All right?"

"All right." Her voice softened. "I'm off to Brazil for the holidays next week. I will miss you. I want you to know pheromones don't travel well by telephone."

He laughed softly. "When this is over, I'll deliver them in person."

"I hope so. Oh, John. I think you should call Znac and ask about the little girl."

"I plan to."

Wood was in a hurry now. He placed a call to Dr. Znac, who answered. He was probably sitting in his office waiting for business.

"Dr. Znac? This is John Wood at the National Academy. I came to see you a while back."

"I remember," Znac said. His voice sounded hollow. "In regard to the Peterson family."

"Tell me, Dr. Znac, how are the children?"

Znac said finally, "The boys are fine." Another pause. Wood immediately knew the reason. "Dr. Wood, Karen is dead. She died a week after you left."

It was Wood's turn to pause. Znac would be feeling on slippery ground because of possible misdiagnosis and treatment, and Wood was not in a position to help him out. "Cause of death?" he asked.

Znac phrased his answer formally. "Karen Peterson passed away unexpectedly. Cause of death appeared to be a delayed

71

toxic reaction to bee venom. The condition is rare but not unknown. It appears in the medical literature."

"Could the symptoms have resembled anything else?"

Znac's voice lost the hollow tone—the coroner in him was coming out. "Strange you should ask that. Yes. In the last days Karen displayed motor dislocation that almost resembled spinal meningitis or . . . or even chemical poisoning. Her skin had a bluish tinge. But her blood showed nothing I could find."

Wood thanked Znac and hung up. He took five or six quick trips to the window and back, and then called Gerston at Columbia. It took almost an hour to find him.

"Your grasshoppers who learned to use DDT—could another insect master a similar stunt?"

"Anything's possible. Which insect?"

"Bees," Wood said.

"Honeybees?"

"That's what I meant, I'm afraid."

Gerston sounded startled. "Let me think. But nobody uses DDT anymore."

"I meant an organophosphate, like methyl parathion."

"Good God! Let's see. Bee stings have three components. A lubricant for a sting, an alkaline substance that softens up the flesh, and the sting itself, which delivers the venom. An organophosphate would be meaningless as a lubricant. In alkaline solution it would be neutralized. It would have to be part of the venom itself."

Wood said, "Suppose an organophosphate were in combination with bee venom, could it be deadly?"

"Hard to say. It might act as a kind of booster, hypertensiating the venom. It would almost have to."

"What would the symptomatology be like?"

"It might look like almost anything. You'd better talk to a

toxicologist. But, John, wouldn't it take a mutated bee to deliver the goods?"

"It probably would."

At the beginning Wood had worried that African bees had entered unseen and in small numbers. If they had, they were precursors of a much greater invasion expected from the South, and it was vital to understand how the bee was faring in North America. He had come away from Maryville concerned that a bee had mutated to a larger size, as suggested by the children, that it made some use of plastic, as verified by the garbage man, and that it was African in origin, as his intuition said. These facts, if true, meant that *adansonii* was indeed modifying itself to fit the American environment.

But now a new angle had presented itself: the possibility of a toxic bee able to use against man the very poisons man unleashed against insects—a feat of incredible biological irony. There was no way of knowing which bees, or how many, possessed this capability, but it seemed to Wood that there had to be a connection between the Maryville bee—possibly African in origin— and the toxic bee. That is, if the toxic bee really existed.

When a scientist lacks physical evidence he will frequently seek proof in statistics. This was the route that Wood took.

The National Academy of Sciences has both a Division of Medical Statistics and an Advisory Center on Toxicology. Neither collected information on bee-sting fatalities, but it turned out that a leading authority on the subject lived in the Washington area.

Recountings of scientific investigations do not always give proper weight to a factor that is not scientific at all—luck. For Wood, finding Dr. George Fine was a lucky stroke. Fine happened to combine unusual skills. With both an M.D. and a

73

Ph.D. in pharmacology, Fine was both an allergist and a toxicologist. He had a private practice out of his office in Georgetown and a consulting relationship with the National Institutes of Health. In his late fifties, he was a withdrawn, cadaverously thin man with a pronounced pallor. His demeanor led Wood to conclude that Fine was extremely cautious, but this, Wood later decided, was a misappraisal. Fine, in fact, was a perfectionist.

He listened to Wood impassively, lit a cigarette, and sat for a long moment saying nothing. At last he sighed, rose, and went to a file, returning with a folder. "I suppose I knew I couldn't sit on this forever," he said reluctantly. "You probably don't realize it, but the Allergy Foundation of America runs a yearly census on fatalities from bites and stings of all kinds. I happen to be chairman of the committee this year. In each state we have an allergist who acts as a reporter, gathers statistics, and sends them in. Eventually they go to the Bureau of Vital Statistics. In a volunteer operation of this kind, nothing is up to date, as you can image. We can run as much as two years behind."

Wood shifted impatiently, and Fine seemed to notice. He opened the folder and gazed at what Wood could see was a row of numbers. Then he went on. "About thirty deaths a year are reported as caused by hymenoptera—bees, wasps, yellow jackets —over half of them by bees. I don't know what to think about these so-called African bees of yours. I'm extremely skeptical. I *do* know for a fact that, from a statistical point of view, there has been a dramatic rise in deaths from honeybee stings. The figures I have are, indeed, two years old. They show that deaths from honeybee stings have doubled."

Wood was not surprised. "Deaths due to anaphylaxis or toxicity?"

"The distinction is meaningless. Anaphylaxis is the result of poisoning. Toxicity covers the whole thing."

"Have you given out these figures?"

"They've been disseminated in bulletin form to allergists. Just gone out, in fact. Other than that, no. For one thing, we're working with very small numbers. Then, I don't have any answers. Are bees turning aggressive, so that they sting more? Are people more sensitive to bee stings than formerly? Is medical reporting getting better? There's no point sounding an alarm until we know where we are."

"Tell me, Dr. Fine, would it be possible to set up a kind of alert? Call it a 'bee watch.' What I had in mind was an information setup, so that your correspondents could inform you more or less at once when a bee sting fatality has occurred."

"It could be done." Fine looked at him curiously. "But why?"

"Well, I hope I'm wrong, but it seems possible that more and more people are going to die of bee stings."

Wood had thus far refrained from telling Fine the notion, improbable as it still seemed, of the toxic bee. He did so now. Fine shook his thin head incredulously. Wood persisted. "If there were such a bee, what would the sting symptoms look like?"

"I guess you mean, what diseases or conditions would the venom mimic? They would have to be in the general area of bee-sting and organophosphate symptomatology. Toxic reactions to bee venom can include trouble in breathing, nervousness, cyanosis, nausea, vomiting, diarrhea, unconsciousness. Organophosphate poisoning symptoms can include chest pains, nervousness, cyanosis, nausea, vomiting, unconsciousness, unconscious defecation. The actual cause of death in both cases is likely to be respiratory failure coupled with a severe cardiovascular reaction. I suppose doctors could confuse the two. Coroners certainly could—they aren't necessarily doctors, you know."

"There's a test, though—right?"

"Yes. For anticholinesterase agents. Do you know about them?"

"Just vaguely."

"Well, acetylcholinesterase, or AChE, terminates transmitter action at the nerve endings when the need for it is finished. If AChE is inactivated, transmission continues, with dire results. The fact that they are anticholinesterase agents is what makes organophosphates so dangerous. Their extreme toxicity led the Germans straight to nerve gases, which are anti-AChE agents. It's a simple matter to test for low levels of AChE, which is the basic clinical means for discovering organophosphate poisoning."

"But in the case of a bee sting, no one would think to make such a test."

Fine rubbed his chin. "They wouldn't, no."

"Or in a heart attack."

"No. I realize what you're driving at. The heart-attack syndrome can produce similar symptoms. What you're suggesting is fearsome. I doubt strongly that it could happen. But you seem like a sensible young man. I will instigate the 'bee watch,' as you call it. It will have to include a closer examination of deaths. Up North the bees hibernate for winter, but in the South they stay outside. I'll get started with my southern allergists. If anything is happening, it ought to show up right away."

At this point Wood, though he lacked final proof, felt he had sufficient evidence to take to Sheldon Hubbard. Outlining his major points in a memo, he presented them at the Monday meeting.

A. A bee swarm sounding suspiciously African in its habits attacked and killed three people in Maryville, New York.
B. In a number of cases, deaths of farm workers in Yolo County, California, were preceded by bee stings.
C. Nationally, the incidence of deaths from bee stings appears to have doubled.

What these things added up to he did not know.

"That, of course, is the problem," Hubbard said, rubbing his hands. "It doesn't add up. Each of your propositions can be challenged as explainable on other grounds." He proceeded to reformulate Wood's propositions:

A. Ordinary wild bees attacked and killed people at Maryville.
B. A number of farm workers in California happened to be stung by bees before dying of other causes.
C. The increased incidence of bee deaths is the result of the mass exodus to the suburbs, where people have more contact with bees, running on lawns with bare feet, etc.

Wood despaired of making headway against Hubbard's blunt logic. "You won't take it seriously, then?"

"I didn't say that. What I'm saying to you is precisely what Willard Lightower would say to me. I don't want to go to him and say 'Here's a three-alarm fire' until I know whether there really is one."

"There is one," Wood said.

Hubbard glared at him. "So *you* say. Listen, if you want to go on gathering information, I won't stop you. But on *your* time. Don't let it interfere with your work."

Wood glared back. It was the closest he had ever come to real anger toward Shelly Hubbard.

Wood then settled down to wait. Nothing happened. There were no bee incidents reported—not a single one.

PART TWO

The
Swarm

7

ENCOUNTERS

The absence of bee incidents in the South confused such concerned scientists as Gerston and Amaral greatly. There seemed no way to account for it except by saying that the Chief Staff Officer of the Division of Environmental Sciences, National Academy of Sciences, a bright, imaginative and pertinacious investigator, had been led from one false conclusion to another, ending with a hypothesis that was completely false.

Those few acquainted with the evidence doubted that this was so. More probably, John Wood believed, a key piece in the puzzle was missing and would be found in due course. In the meantime nothing could be done but wait. Wood was unhappily convinced that the bee incidents would begin again in the spring. They would start sooner if the spring was early and warm, as meteorologists predicted.

Henry David, the beekeeper, returned from the South in March. The maple trees and dandelions had not started to flower yet, but they would soon from the look of things. It had been a winter like 1973—warm, with hardly any snow, and once again spring would be early. David wondered if the climate was changing—everything else seemed to be.

Having let the new bees feed for several days to recover from the trip, he set about introducing them to his hives. The new queens, surrounded by knots of workers, were in small wire cages, each with a plug of hard candy inserted in the side. If the new queens had been set loose without formality, the bees would have balled them at once because of their protectiveness toward the queen they already had. By the time bees on both sides of the candy plug had eaten through it, the workers of the hive would have gotten used to the smell of the new queen. The problem was an old one. Usually the laws of the bee kingdom ruled that only one queen prevailed. Two queens would fight to the death, and this was the only time the queen used her sting. If the bees had a problem, David sometimes thought, that was it—the regal one. The very insistence on a single queen mother made the bees vulnerable if she died.

As a practical matter, the law was not always followed to the letter. Sometimes, if the colony was large enough, it would accept two queens, each ruling half of the kingdom and never venturing upon the other half. If the reigning queen was young and vigorous, David would sometimes hope for the best and permit the ruling queen to stay. Old queens, however, he destroyed, pacifying the hive with his smoker and removing the queen with his bare fingers.

This was the first change David noticed. The bees were abnormally resistant to smoke. Usually, a few puffs quieted them, but this spring he had to use his smoker repeatedly to make them settle down. He was looking for the queen in the first hive when he saw the giants. They must have emerged from the brood cells in late February or early March, when he was away. These bees were black and orange and nearly an inch long—twice the size of the ordinary workers. Not all the bees in the hive were giants, but there were enough to make David understand that something outside his long experience had occurred.

Henry David did not have a telephone. If he had, he would have notified Dr. Znac in Maryville. Znac would know whom to report the finding to. He thought about driving into town, but he was tired from the trip. He decided to wait a little and see what happened. Perhaps these giant bees would prove to be enormous producers of honey. Then he would have something really important to report.

Perry Goodall brought new bees down in March from his house in Connecticut to replenish his urban hive, half of which had swarmed. These new bees were different. They seemed to have undergone, he quipped, a "bee change." They buzzed a lot. They flew about seemingly erratically and rolled in bunches in the backyard. Sometimes they seemed harder to approach, though they were still amenable to the beard stunt. Sometimes he had a strange feeling that they were angry about something. The children were frightened of them—one of the girls said the bees had become larger. Goodall doubted it. He thought once about taking some bees to the Museum of Natural History for inspection, but ended by laughing at himself. Who but a fool would be frightened of bees?

Spring advanced inexorably, with record temperatures and a good deal of rain.

Mrs. Adele Terrace, of Oyster Bay, Long Island, gave her maid Thursday afternoons off. The maid, she discovered one Thursday, had forgotten to put out the garbage, and Mrs. Terrace carried the bags to the pails behind the high wooden fence.

Mrs. Terrace saw bees buzzing around a can whose lid was partially ajar. She picked up a piece of newspaper to shoo them away and received in return a single sting on her hand. Mrs. Terrace had never been stung by a bee before and felt outraged. She called her physician, who came at once. He knew Mrs. Terrace.

Still, although Mrs. Terrace frequently suffered from ills the doctor diagnosed as imaginary, he was puzzled this time. The finger swelled and so did Mrs. Terrace's face. He supposed she had a bee-sting allergy, but she had received only one sting, and a light one at that. She was in bed for three days.

At the Tuesday bridge game Mrs. Terrace told her friends about the incident. She wanted a local ordinance banning bees from Oyster Bay. "I say, kill the bees," she insisted. "They're up to no good, and will only end by lowering property values. None of us wants that."

A Wisconsin woman hung towels on the line to dry. How white they looked in the sunshine!

About to go indoors, she noticed a clot of bees around the water dripping from the towels. A few bees flew into the garage or over the back stoop, returning to the clot. She had a hunch they were planning something, like settling down on her property. Taking a broom, she tried to scare them away, but the bees began flying in circles above her head. Frightened, she ran inside, but left the kitchen door open. Her husband found her body that evening. She had been badly stung by bees, but the coroner was sure she had died from shock. Taking no chances, he called in a local allergist to have a look.

Drunk, he walked along the dark Rhode Island highway, waving his arms and singing, aimed for the cabin in which his wife waited and would continue to wait. Once he staggered onto the road by mistake and narrowly missed being smeared by a truck. Alarmed in spite of the booze, he crashed into the bushes, intending to find a place to lie down and sleep it off. He stopped to take a leak, still singing. The song changed to a scream. His body was not discovered for several days.

The young woman had been warned against hitchhiking—in fact, the laws of Colorado expressly forbade it. But not for the reason that sent her into a coma on the side of the road. An ambulance rushed her to a county hospital, where an alert physician noted the welts on her scalp underneath her hair. He took a chance; adrenalin would have been just the wrong treatment for overdose. Within minutes the young woman revived.

Three days later, having reached California, she collapsed and died without warning. The medical examiner was confounded. The symptoms resembled encephalitis, but he could find no trace of the disease. Then, in her wallet he found a card from a Colorado hospital warning that the girl was allergic to bee stings. He telephoned an allergist.

In California the cultists emerged early in the warm spring. This colony had located in the Big Sur, on the rocks by the sea, where on weekends it practiced a combination of encounter techniques, sexual liberation and just plain nudity.

Newspaper attention fastened on the nudity angle, with little thought as to why bees attacked. The nudists lying on the rocks had covered themselves with lotions and oils, and perhaps the sweet aroma brought the bee swarm. At once a function of clothing became apparent, the protection of private parts. There were six people on the rocks, and instead of fighting the bees with their hands, they clutched their most vulnerable areas and backed off. This action saved four of them. It did not help the two who fell off the cliff.

The "bee watch" had been established nationwide by now; in Washington, Fine put two more marks in his pad, followed by a question mark.

In southern Vermont the commune was entering its third year with its fundamental problem unresolved. Try as they did, its members could not find a way to make a living.

Farming in the rocky ground had been a disaster. Logging had proved beyond its resources, and having tried producing

85

maple syrup and sugar, the commune knew why the industry did not flourish in the state—returns were just too low. This summer the commune had a new idea.

The preceding fall several members of the group had attended a session on beekeeping at Cornell University. They had been taught the necessary techniques, and now, in possession of a hundred hives of bees, they were ready to go.

The bees had been bought from a nearby beekeeper who was quitting the business; he did not say why. In fact, he seemed eager to sell them his equipment and bees for a reasonable price. The deal had no sooner been made—with almost the last of the commune's money—when the beekeeper brought the bees to them by truck. He seemed in a hurry to depart.

A few days later the weather turned warm and the bees came out of the hives. The group turned out to watch them. Some swarms, however, did not emerge. To get them out, some of the boys began beating upon the wooden hives with sticks.

The recalcitrant bees did indeed emerge—in a bad humor. Three more marks appeared on Fine's tally sheet.

It was Saturday again, and Dr. David P. Znac sat alone in his office. Business was bad. A new clinic had opened down the road, and besides, as he knew, there was a rumor around that Znac had been guilty of a serious misdiagnosis in the case of the Peterson girl, and might lose his job as coroner. Znac thought bitterly that he might be the first doctor in history to go on welfare.

He held the bees responsible. They had tricked him in some way, and he wanted to get back at them. It occurred to him suddenly to go on a bee hunt. The hour was early and there was nothing to keep him in town except the bottle.

Taking up a bee tree was hard on the hunter but harder on the bees. Early spring, before the foliage had grown thick and when the bees were hungry, was the best time of the year. A colony that had survived the winter was bound to be strong. You tracked the bees to their hive and emblazoned your initials on the bee tree. This established the hive as yours. Having secured permission of the owner—which was never difficult—you returned with a helper or two in the fall. You needed a veil and gloves then, because the bees fought bitterly for their home. When the tree came down, you invaded the hive and took the honey, perhaps a hundred pounds or more. With luck you might capture the hive, but mostly, spent and demoralized, the bees dispersed in the woods to die.

In these parts bee hunting was an old sport—Znac's bee box had belonged to his father. The equipment required was simple. Not even a veil and gloves were required for the first operation, because bees in the spring were peaceable. Besides the box, you needed only some honey, a watch, a piece of honeycomb, a little anise, a camel's-hair brush, a little jar of paint and patience. Sometimes you could track a bee tree in an hour, but sometimes it took two days.

Znac had nobody to say good-bye to—his wife had left him, his children were grown and gone. Taking his equipment, he hung an *Out to Lunch* sign on the door and drove to the woods. Then he started to hunt.

The first step was to catch a bee. He searched, found one taking nectar in a patch of flowers, and caught it with a quick upward motion of the box, shutting the lid. The bee box—about the size of a cigar box—had two compartments, with a movable slide between them to permit access from one compartment to the other. Each compartment had a glass window that could be shuttered over. Znac opened the window of the rear compartment and the bee went in there, attracted by the light. Znac now closed the slide between the compartments, and the front section was free.

He repeated the process until a dozen bees crowded the rear section. Then, in the front compartment he placed the comb smeared with honey laced with a little anise. The bees liked the liquor, but you had to be careful not to use too much or you got them drunk. Moving the center slide, he let a few bees into the front section, then closed it again. Finally he covered the windows in the box, placed the box on a stump, opened the front hatch, lay on the ground, and watched.

The honey-loaded bees came out, flying in slowly expanding circles and figure eights, until all flew off in the same direction, with Znac rolling on his back as he tried to follow them with his eyes. He repeated the exercise until all the bees in the box were gone. Now he had to wait.

He recognized the shrill sound of the returning honeybee instantly, separating it from the other noises of the forest. The bee found the box, darted around it, disappeared, and whizzed back, hovering like a helicopter over the comb, until at last it descended. Znac sighed with relief; the beeline was started. This time, though, he took the camel's-hair brush, and as the bee was feeding, daubed it quickly with a spot of white paint. Other bees followed, and he daubed them too, glancing at his watch.

He could imagine the scene at the hive, high in a tree and probably hidden from view. This early in the year food would not be plentiful; the scouts, now confident of the location of food, would be reporting it. They would do this by means of the waggle, or honey dance, moving in a circle if the food was less than one hundred yards away, and in a gradually fuller figure eight if it was farther, pointing the precise direction with the line joining the two loops of the figure eight. Waggling their tails as they danced, they could indicate the exact location of food as far as two miles distant. Following these directions, other bees would find the food, fill up on it, and aim unerringly back to the hive, a calculation that for a human would require a stop watch, a compass and vector calculus.

In ten minutes the first marked bee returned—a big fellow, Znac now noticed. Znac figured the honey dance had taken about two minutes. A bee flies at about fourteen miles an hour. That meant the hive was approximately a mile away.

By this time he had established the general line of the bee's flight back to the hive. It was time to move. Holding the box crowded with bees, he moved about a hundred yards to the left and opened the box again. Soon he had established a new bee-line, which, when triangulated with the first, gave him a fair idea of where the bee tree was.

He had been fortunate so far. He might have failed to find a bee, or the bee might have refused the honey or might not have returned to the box. But locating the tree was not easy. Hour after hour he caught bees, fed them, marked them, and changed locations, following the bees along until at last he looked up and saw the hole in the tree with a glittering of wings around it.

At that moment Znac realized the bee trail had taken him close to where the Peterson family had been attacked. Perhaps he had known it all along. Conceivably, he could still have escaped, but he chose instead to walk to the tree. He had just finished blazing his initials on the bark when a roar filled the woods.

Two days later, in Washington, Dr. Fine wondered if a bee-sting suicide was conceivable. There had already been a bee incident at Maryville. Who, in that vicinity, would deliberately hunt a wild hive except a fool? And a medical doctor was not likely to be a fool; at least, Fine hoped not.

He had gathered enough evidence to prove that deaths from bee stings, though the symptoms did not always square with the classic symptomatology, were up—and sharply. The evidence was no longer inconclusive. It was Friday. On Monday he would talk to John Wood to say that his allergists had assembled the evidence. Wanted now was the killer.

8

IDENTIFICATION

Dreams have often been interpreted as signposts to the future, signals sent by the unconscious mind as a foreshadowing of things to come. The nearer John Wood moved toward the crisis that engulfed him the more frequent the bee dreams became, until his nights were tortured by them.

On Saturday, April 2, Wood accepted Hubbard's invitation to play golf at the Chevy Chase Country Club. The place was too stuffy for Wood's taste, but Hubbard did not leave much room to refuse. Every so often he dragooned Wood into golf on the grounds that he lacked a partner, although Wood always suspected golf to be part of Hubbard's long-range campaign to show the younger scientist who was boss. Hubbard was the better player, but on good days Wood could keep up.

"How's that for an old zoologist?" Hubbard said, watching his drive carry the ball over the fairway and onto the green. He wiped his round pink face with a handkerchief and beamed.

Determined, Wood addressed the ball with every inch of strength he had. It was a good drive, except that it began to veer dangerously to the left, ending in a clump of trees. Wood scowled.

I'm just tense, he told himself. The bee thing is getting to me. Waiting, waiting, for what I'm not quite sure.

The two men wheeled their carts to the next tee, and Wood went off to find his ball. Unable to locate it at the edge of the copse, he struggled through some bushes, furious with himself. It would take him two shots, probably, to get on the green again if he found the ball at all. Then, in a pile of leaves, he saw it. At the same moment he heard the sound.

If he hadn't been alert for the sound he probably would not have isolated this particular thrum from the other insect noises in the copse; it was barely audible. But he knew he had heard it before. It was a high-pitched buzz, almost like that which a small machine would make. Of course—in the clearing at Maryville!

Then he saw it. Hovering over a cluster of spring wild flowers was a honeybee—the streamlined shape left no doubt about that. Black with orange markings, it was by far the largest bee Wood had ever seen.

Stealthily he backed out of the clearing, forced his way through the bushes and ran to Hubbard at the hole.

"Penalty, huh?" the beetle laughed.

"Shelly, give me your glove. Quick."

Wood, right-handed, wore a light leather glove on his left hand; Hubbard, left-handed, wore his golf glove on his right hand. Hubbard blinked at him and removed the glove. Without waiting for questions John ran back to the trees. Hubbard started to follow, but Wood yelled, "Stay back."

If he was about to confront an African swarm, he wanted to face it alone. A pulse beat in his temple and his hands shook but Wood could not back off now.

He almost hoped the bee would be gone but he found it, proboscis buried deep in a flower. His body prickled dryly from the memory of stings. He inched forward warily, fighting his own reluctant muscles, glancing to see if other bees were in the vicinity. This one appeared to be by itself.

When Wood's gloved hands were poised on either side of the flower, the bee, as if alerted, suddenly emerged, about to take off. Wood clapped his hands together, hard but not hard enough —as if fear had put a drag on his reactions. Just before its death the bee managed to use its barb. The sting carried through the light leather of the glove into Wood's palm. Pain stabbed to his elbow.

"God," he gasped.

Staggering a little, he fought his way out of the copse and onto the green, where Hubbard waited, leaning on his driver. Seeing Wood's face, he gawked.

Wood showed Hubbard the dead bee he carried in his gloved palm.

"Son of a bitch," Hubbard said. He took the bee. "What is it, a carpenter bee?"

Hubbard was not an easy man to convince. Wood removed the glove and showed the beetle his wounded palm. "I believe carpenter bees don't sting," he managed to say.

Hubbard stared long and hard at the bee. "Whatever it is, I don't like it."

In the clubhouse Wood threw up, and then he felt all right, except for his hand, which he bathed in cold water. If the bee was toxic, he had evidently gotten a low dosage—either that or sensitivity varied, he reasoned. Meantime Hubbard called Birch at the Smithsonian, who said he would wait. It was decided that Wood would go alone—both men were not needed. Wood said he was up to it.

He was grinning insanely as he drove the Volks downtown. Whatever was to happen, he had on this day accomplished something important to himself. He had conquered his bee phobia.

The naturalist placed his amber-framed glasses low on his nose and stared at the specimen, lips pursed.

"It's a giant honeybee, no doubt about that," he said. "Which family it's descended from is another matter. Identification from dead specimens can be hard, sometimes impossible. *Apis mellifera* is represented in the Old World by numerous subspecies, several of which have been introduced to the New World, where a great deal of interbreeding has taken place. The same has happened in Brazil with the Africans. Still, structural characteristics, color features, and size of specimens can be sufficiently diagnostic in their aggregate to make reliable identification possible. But no one characteristic or feature can be counted on to clinch the answer. In all, there are more than fifty characteristics to look for, if you care to wait." He pulled sharply on his ear. "I *will* say that this is the goddamnedest bee I ever saw."

For the next hour Bill Birch worked in almost utter silence. First he mounted the bee on a pin thrust through the forward part of the body, just right of center. From metal cabinets he removed clear plastic boxes containing mounted and labeled bees, which he compared with the specimen, occasionally taking the unidentified bee to the window for a better look. Once in a while he looked up references in a thick book.

Birch then put the bee under what he said was a binocular dissecting microscope, rolling it over and over, tabulating characteristics on a pad. Finally he dissected a wing from the specimen and placed it between microscope slides. The slides went into a downward projector that showed the wing image on graph paper beneath. Birch marked the wing measurements and made a series of dots. The graph was then compared with other graphs he took from a folder. "Come over here," Birch said to Wood at last.

The naturalist turned a knob and the image below the projector grew larger. Wood noted that the wing was heavily veined and had curious hooklike terminations. "There are eighteen vein intersections in a bee's fore wing," Birch said, "and a number of angles, which I have measured with a protractor. These hooks are called hamuli. The general configuration of the bee— large wings as compared with body size, the length of the legs and the tongue, the number and color of the dorsal rings on the abdomen—told me something. But the vein structure and especially the large number of hamuli, which tie the wings together, did it. I'm satisfied. Yes, there is no doubt about it. I thought at first it might be the giant Indian honeybee, but it isn't. Only one bee group has a wing configuration of this kind. I could run the taxonomy out on a computer, but I don't need to. This big fellow is *adansonii*, the African honeybee."

The two men stood looking at each other. "But the size," Wood said at last.

"This is a hybrid—no, I have to say mutated version. *Adansonii*'s cousin, if you like. Where did you find it?"

"Practically right here in Washington—Chevy Chase."

Birch stared and said quietly, "So it's gotten in."

"Yes. The question is, how many of these things are here?"

"No. I think the question is, how long have they been here?" Birch corrected him. "In its pure form *Apis mellifera adansonii Latreille*—to use its full name—is about ten percent smaller than domestic bees. Its small stature gives it agility, making escape from enemies easier. This bee has sacrificed agility for some other survival characteristic—I have no idea what. Of course, it could be a freak, a single mutant. But that's unlikely."

"Yes."

"And the mutation is almost bound to have happened here, not in Brazil. Giants there would have been reported or spotted coming in. It has to have been here a while. This sort of change can't happen overnight."

"How many years would it take, Dr. Birch?"

"Oh, as a guess, I'd say on the order of five. The Africans reproduce faster than our queens. Their queens mature in a few days less. Let's say three generations every summer. Maybe that's pushing it, but maybe not. Yes, five years ought to allow for this big insect to emerge. There would have to be a lot of them. The African queens lay maybe double the number of eggs that our queens do, therefore they swarm more. Their fantastic population growth is another survival characteristic, because their enemies deplete them. But here they wouldn't have their classic enemies, and the buildup would be unbelievable."

"All the Afro-American hybrids wouldn't have to be giants, would they?"

"Definitely not," Birch said. "Every generation would be in a different stage of transition from one form to another. By the fifth year many bees might have some but not all of the characteristics of the new bee. They might be aggressive, say, but not appreciably larger in size than domestic bees. But sooner or later they'd all go the same route—toward this new insect." He held up the pin carrying Wood's bee.

"New insect?" Wood said.

"We discover about six thousand new insects a year. This will have to be classified as one of them. It's a mutation of great importance in terms of pedigree. It needs a new name. Traditionally, the name of the discoverer of a new insect has his name attached to it. How about *Apis mellifera Woodii?* No—we should keep the African family name. *Adansonii Wood.*"

"No," John Wood said. He was thinking of the Peterson family. "I'd like to name it after a town—Maryville."

"*A.M. adansonii Maryvillis* it is," Birch said, holding the bee up to the light. It was a prophetic choice of nomenclature.

The Monday meeting between Hubbard and Wood took place in Willard Lightower's office. The president of the National Academy of Sciences was a noted administrator as well as physicist, quick to move when he had the facts. His square face was impassive as he listened to Shelly Hubbard's presentation.

"It appears," Hubbard said from deep in a leather wing chair, "that we are confronted with still another accidental import, this one equipped with a nasty disposition and a special dislike for human beings. It's our old friend the African honeybee, which has been spreading in South America. How it got in I plain don't know, and how long it has been in I don't know

95

either. I do know that there has been a rash of incidents throughout the country involving hostile bees, and the connection must be more than coincidental. The bee apparently exists in many areas of the country, but changed from its South American version. It is larger—and we have learned that increased-size mutations often lead to heightened aggressiveness. A second and really quite ominous finding is that this new bee can be toxic and may be able to cause death with a single sting."

Lightower looked at the photograph of the President of the United States over the fireplace. "What would you have me do?" he asked slowly.

It was Wood's turn. "We believe there ought to be a working unit set up immediately to study this phenomenon and recommend action. Speed is essential. There's no reason to think the Africans have infiltrated the American population—the invaders probably still exist in isolated pockets. But if the African bees do become dominant, the implications are very grave."

Lightower said, "The bee—or an earlier version of it—might have come in undetected over the Mexican border. If some did, others will too. This group might be the advance guard of a mass invasion from the south."

"Invasions have happened before," Hubbard said. "Painted lady butterflies coming in from Mexico in the late eighteen-hundreds made a cloud a mile wide that passed overhead continuously for three straight days. There must have been trillions of them."

"Of course, the resistance of the domestic bee population counts for something, doesn't it?" Lightower asked.

Wood said, "But the introduction of Africans into American hives would soften that resistance."

"The revenge of the Africans," Lightower mused. "Africans armed with poison darts. Unprovoked stingings, mass attacks, casualties—can you imagine how people would react? They'd just kill off all bees regardless of what they are. Already there is a growing intolerance for bees. People are frightened of them, as reflected in local ordinances against beekeeping. We have one here in Washington. And the press will have a field day. People don't realize that bees are absolutely vital to the economy. They account for the pollination of five or six billion dollars' worth of crops a year. And let me tell you something even you boys don't know. It's classified, but I'll reveal it anyway. At Oak Ridge a large area was subjected to radiation that cleared it of all animal life, including insects. Projections were then made as to the future of plant life without insects, especially bees. It showed that not only would some forms of plant life die off but that in the end there would be no vegetation to speak of at all."

Lightower stopped, as though to let his point sink in. "Okay, I think you have something. Get a group together. But keep it secret. If your work is known at this stage, it could start a panic. Don't use the word 'bee' in the title."

"How about simply capital B Group?" Wood said.

B Group it was.

Two mornings later, on Wednesday, April 6, six men were seated around Hubbard's conference table. In addition to Wood and Hubbard there were McAllister, Krim, Gerston and Fine. Together they represented the best in their disciplines.

Hubbard chaired. He had scribbled a few notes on a pad and glanced at them, a glint in his deep-set eyes. "I know you're anxious to get down to business, but before we do, there is something to settle. It's a matter of nomenclature. How do we identify the enemy? Is it to be 'her' or 'him'? Bees are predominantly female insects, but I can't help thinking of war as a male occupation. Let's call the enemy 'him.' "

The group concurred, though Wood smiled slightly.

Wood added, "Besides, it's a mistake to think of him in traditional terms. The Africans are just as much the enemy of the domestic bee as they are our own."

"Agreed," McAllister said in his high-pitched voice. "I think one of our first steps ought to be to make contact with the Department of Agriculture. USDA ought to get out a circular to beekeepers warning them against bees that act or look strange. They ought to be reported."

Gerston stretched his long arms. "But not destroyed. We're going to need specimens. Lots of them."

"Live ones," Krim said, his voice sounding muffled, as if it passed through his beard. "I can't do genetic work with a dead insect."

Staring at the nervous little man, Wood had to remind himself he was one of the world's leading geneticists.

"I need live insects for toxicity studies too," Fine remarked.

"The Africans will show up at apiaries. Don't worry, we'll bring some back alive," McAllister said.

Gerston said, "Sooner or later we'll have to start killing them. I suppose pesticides are out?"

"Only as a last resort," Wood said. "The politics of DDT make it almost impossible to use. People are dead set against it."

"Besides," Fine said, "if this bee has indeed learned to metabolize organophosphates, one would only be giving it exactly what it wants."

"The best defense is still to change the gene pool," Krim said.

"Perhaps," Wood answered. "But we're still going to need the most sophisticated control techniques available."

"Maybe juvenile growth inhibitors will do the job," McAllister said.

"We could go the screwworm-fly route and drop sterilized males," Gerston advised.

Hubbard looked at the paper on which he had been making notes. "We must have information on the biology of the bee—

its distribution, rate of reproduction, toxicity, genetic makeup, susceptibility to various means of control. We need also to understand the feasibility of line-rearing our own bees—we may have to breed our own bees to use against the Africans. That means a facility of some kind, with a lab. Maybe a big facility. I'll see what I can do about designing one. The question is where to put it." He looked at Wood. "It's premature, I know, but why don't you nose around? Just in case."

Wood was thinking that Sheldon Hubbard had a mechanical challenge before him and could not resist it. In a previous experiment he had proved the feasibility of rearing beetles for use against other beetles. Now he wanted to do it with bees. "All right," he said.

Hubbard took a new sheet of paper, scribbled on it, and passed it to Wood, who sat on his right.

B GROUP
Line Responsibilities

Facility requirements	*Sheldon Hubbard*
	John Wood
Testing, Behavioral characteristics	*F. W. McAllister*
Genetics	*Walter Krim*
Toxicology, Immunology,	*George Fine*
Epidemiology	
Specimen collection	*Robert Gerston*
Radiation sterilization techniques	

Hubbard said, "One man in this group is not overworked." He gazed at Wood. "We need a coordinator. Why don't you take that job, John?"

Wood said, "Okay by me." Taking the paper, he added the job to the list and passed it on.

When the list reached Fine, his pale face objected. "It's too

99

much. It will be hard work for me. I'm not as young as the rest of you, and a real bee-sting antitoxin has never been developed, much less one for a bizarre venom—if this proves to be the case. On the spread question, better find yourself an epidemiologist."

"Anybody know a good one?" Hubbard asked.

Wood hesitated, then drawled, "I do. A woman. She's a Brazilian and knows a lot about our African friends."

Gerston said, "I'm all for having a woman. Even better if she's pretty. Any problems with the Official Secrets Act?"

Wood looked embarrassed. "I don't think so, no. I checked it out."

"Uh-huh," Hubbard murmured gleefully.

It was noon. Wood realized he was now the coordinator. "Let's break and meet again tomorrow. By then everybody ought to have a report on how he proposes to do his job. In case any of you thinks we have plenty of time," he said seriously, "you could be wrong."

The entries on Wood's personal long-distance telephone bills were a guide to Maria's movements—Davis, Calif., Davis, Calif., Davis, Calif., São Paulo, Brazil, São Paulo, Brazil, São Paulo, Brazil, Davis, Calif., Davis, Calif., etc. This time he called her on the office phone.

"I found an African," he said simply.

There was silence on the line. "You mean a live one, there in Washington?" she said, as though not really believing him.

"Yes. Now we have the proof we've been waiting for. We're going into action. Can you shake loose?"

"You mean come?" she said excitedly. She thought a moment. "It will take me a few days."

"I can't wait."

"Should I bring anything?"

"Just your pheromones."

Then, in his tiny office, Wood placed a series of calls, using

Lightower's authority. That afternoon found him at the Pentagon.

Brigadier General Thaddeus W. Slater, Jr., U.S.A., of the Advanced Research Projects Agency of the Department of Defense, was polite but unhelpful. Wood wished that Hubbard had come with him—the beetle carried weight. But Hubbard was occupied in designing the bee facility.

A beefy, red-faced man, Slater reminded Wood of a British sergeant major circa 1890. "Bees, you say. I remember a movie about driver ants, starring Charlton Heston, I think. Anything like that?"

"Nothing like that," Wood said.

"I have to tell you that it would take a national emergency to pry one of our joints loose. My bosses, the four-star generals, look at military property as their own."

"What's happening at Fort Detrick?" Wood asked.

Slater looked at him with curiosity. "Detrick's stopped doing biological warfare, and there's some unused space and lab equipment. There's even an army communications center. But you'd need the authority of the President to get it."

"Well, we'll see," Wood said.

"Do that." Slater touched Wood's arm at the door. "A thought occurs to me. Do you know that bees have been used in warfare almost since it started? The Greeks and Phoenicians catapulted beehives at the enemy. Bees were used for defense— medieval towns dropped bees from the walls on the attackers. If a bee got inside a man's armor, you can imagine the effect. In the Russo-Japanese War the Japanese used bees for sending messages—they'd attach tiny papers to them. The Germans in East Africa released bees against the British in World War One."

Wood turned around. "What do you have in mind? Sounds as though you've done a feasibility study."

"Correct. We sent a team of entomologists to the Far East to investigate the possibility of using chemicals to set off beehives against the Vietcong, who have been known to use swarms against the South Vietnamese. I believe the boys wrote a paper.* We finally decided it wasn't practicable, even if bees wouldn't be ruled out as a weapon under the biological warfare provisions of the Geneva Convention. That's a murky area. But these bees of yours—sounds like a couple of million dropped by plane would do real damage."

Wood said, "They may do real damage, General Slater, *here*."

The meeting on Friday started just after lunch. Hubbard went first, with the others scheduled to follow—though as it turned out only Hubbard was destined to give a report that day.

Sheldon Hubbard unrolled a long sheet of butcher paper on the conference table. Sketched there was what looked like the letter E.

"This," he said, rubbing his hands, "is a design for a bee factory. It's easy to assemble—prefab modular housing units for the greenhouses will do the trick. The facility is designed for assembly-line-rearing queens, drones and workers—assuming we had need for all three. Queens—virgins, I imagine—will be brought from the South and fertilized here." He touched the vertical shaft of the E. "The eggs they lay are moved—by conveyor belt, that should be easy—along these three rows for the number of days required." He pointed to the horizontal shaft of the E. "Finally they emerge at the end as adult bees. And every day a new lot of bees begins on the line. So you have a continuous laying and maturation system, just as occurs in a beehive."

* R. A. Morse, D. A. Shearer, R. Boch and A. W. Benton, "Observations on Alarm Substances in the Genus Apis," *Journal of Apicultural Research* (2): 113–118 (1967).

"How wide is the conveyor belt?"

"Figure six feet. Standard."

Krim began calculating quickly, using whole numbers to the tenth power. McAllister had a smile on his face. Krim looked up and tugged on his beard. "Quite a factory, Shelly. Do you know how long it will have to be?"

Hubbard's expression was glum. "How long?"

"About eight hundred miles." They all smiled, except Hubbard. "That'll be quite a conveyor belt. Think we can get it built by Christmas?"

McAllister was cackling. "You must be thinking about beetles, Shelly. There are four thousand worker bee cells per square foot."

Hubbard looked shattered. "How long does that make the factory?"

Krim said quickly, "Only eight miles long."

Hubbard said, as if to change the subject, "Well, where will the facility be located?"

Wood said, "I've an idea—Fort Detrick, Maryland, where the BW research labs used to be. The setup would be ideal."

McAllister glanced quickly at him. "How do you know?"

"I checked around," Wood said. He paused, then added, "Besides, I used to work there."

Except for Hubbard, who knew about Wood's background, they stared at him in surprise and even horror.

"You *worked* there?" Krim said.

"Yes. I was assigned to the BioLabs during my military service."

Further reactions were cut short by the arrival of the divisional secretary. She seemed embarrassed. "I'm sorry to break in. I keep my radio on softly when I type. You gentlemen are conferring about bees. I thought you would want to know that bees are attacking a town in New York State."

9

THE SWARM

Testimony before the House Environmental Preparedness Subcommittee, July 6, throws light on the events at Maryville.

REP. JAMES WATKINS, D. ORE., CHMN. Mr. Himmel, you are, or were, a sanitation officer at Maryville, New York?

RUDOLPH HIMMEL. I am, sir.

WATKINS. We are trying to determine if a national emergency exists, so please weigh your answers carefully.

HIMMEL. Yes, sir.

WATKINS. Was there any warning before the bees attacked the town?

HIMMEL. Nope. Not exactly.

WATKINS. Please explain.

HIMMEL. Last fall, family up there was attacked and parents killed by bees. Then Dr. Znac, our coroner, got it in the forest. At the dump . . .

WATKINS. Go on.

HIMMEL. At the dump—I mean refuse-disposal system—been seeing a lot of bees. Clouds of them. I kept away from them. Queer bees, they was. Big [*deleted*]. Sorry.

WATKINS. Strike the profanity from the records, please. Continue.

HIMMEL. Seen bees before, feeding on fruit, broken honey jars—you know. But these bees like plastic too.

WATKINS. You have an open dump?

HIMMEL. People come and throw garbage in it. Hours are nine to six on weekdays, nine to twelve on Sundays.

WATKINS. I don't plan to use it myself. [*Laughter*] What would bees be doing with plastic?

HIMMEL. Don't know. They dig away at Styrofoam with their . . . claws.

WATKINS. "Mandibles" is the word, I guess. What would they be doing with Styrofoam?

HIMMEL. I don't know. Taking it home. Building something.

WATKINS. Why do you say "building"?

HIMMEL. What else would they do with it?

WATKINS. Please explain the exact circumstances leading to the attack.

HIMMEL. Well, like I said, the folks in town were nervous. There seemed to be more and more bees around all the time. It was Friday, about noon, during school lunch hour. The kids were throwing rocks.

The bee tree in the town square had been there as long as anyone in Maryville remembered. Some said the nest had been there when the town was founded, over two hundred years before, but the tree might have been unoccupied part of the time. The hole was high enough in the tree so that you would never have seen it unless you knew where to look, and you could have lived in Maryville without being aware of the hive at all. But everybody was.

No one knew whether it happened by accident or as an act of revenge. Of course there had been the newspaper stories about bee attacks, and here at home the tragedies of the Petersons and Dr. Znac. When the stone entered the hole the kids at the base of the tree stood silent and uncertain, as though they had dared the gods and must risk the consequences.

Nothing happened immediately. Then the tree began to emit a kind of whine, as though the bee hole were its mouth—

Ziiiiiiiii. An endless black jet streamed from the hive and rose into the sky.

Townspeople came out of the shops to look, staring up in awe. Nobody could recall having seen bees fly this way, turning, wheeling, rising, dipping, like a huge kite or a magic carpet. It was a fantastic sight, and they stared.

All at once the bee cloud descended. A roar, faint at first, then overwhelming, filled the square. *Zuuuuuuuuummmm.* ZUUUUUUUUUMMMM. Bees dropped like hailstones. Howling dogs ran and collided. The people in the square dashed for cover.

Some were lucky, some not. A woman made it to her car, and sat in terror behind closed windows as bees crashed against the windshield like small stones. Covering his eyes, a man careened into the plate-glass window of a haberdashery, cracking it. He remained there, impaled.

The sound of the bees seemed to rouse other hives. From the woods around town bee swarms appeared on the horizon like squadrons of minuscule bombers on a mission.

The bees seemed to concentrate on the ice cream parlor. People ran in and locked the door behind them, while, outside, a man with bees clustered on his face and arms pounded the plate-glass door in vain before he staggered off, screaming. A few bees had entered with the people, and there was pandemonium inside the parlor as people tried to kill the bees, upsetting glasses and dishes as they flailed around them with newspapers and magazines. Bees drummed against the thick windows, leaving clumps of liquid and hair.

Perhaps those in the ice cream parlor might have weathered the bee storm. But a foolish and frightened customer exited the back way, leaving the door open, and bees entered. They banged into the shiny pots on the rack. Stung, the short-order chef upset a fat-filled skillet on the grill, and a fire started. Flames, smoke and ranging bees forced the people in the ice cream parlor out into the street, where the massed bees hovered.

Tim and Randy Peterson had been among the knot of boys at the tree, one of whom had cast the stone. The two ran to Thelma Billings' house, two blocks away. The noise from the square was audible and appeared to be getting louder. Thelma closed the doors and windows, but soon bees were knocking against them. Thelma did the one thing she could think of—she put the boys on the bed, lay down beside them, pulled the blankets over their heads, and prayed.

The first bees entered through the chimney, and then came the tinkle of broken window glass.

Bees roared over a silent town.

It was late afternoon when a chartered plane brought Wood and Gerston to the nearest airport, at Wappingers Falls, New York, where a rental car waited. About a half mile outside town a state-police barricade stopped them, but Wood showed his NAS credentials and they were allowed to proceed. On the outskirts of Maryville they put on veils and protective clothing, but the precaution proved needless.

An unearthly quiet hung over Maryville. A neat row of bodies, faces covered, lined one side of the square. A few tortured shapes still lay in the street. A crust of bees covered the road, crunching under the tires. Rolling down the window of the station wagon, Wood motioned to a state trooper who carried a cyanide gun. "All over?"

"Gone. For good, I reckon." He gestured toward the second-growth timber at the edge of town. His face was gray.

"How many dead?" Gerston asked.

"Fourteen, and still counting. Many others are stung bad." He watched a woman being carried on a stretcher from a store. "Fifteen."

107

Not all the bees were dead. Some, plainly spent, huddled in helpless clumps on the street. Gerston got out, and Wood drove quickly to Thelma Billings' house. He found what he had feared. When he returned to the square he said to the trooper, "Eighteen."

They were sawing the magnificent elm in the square, as if to punish it for harboring the enemy. The tree fell with a crash, breaking at the spot where the hive was. Wood went over. Underneath the sticky masses of honey and comb a bluish-yellow substance glinted in the late afternoon sun. Wood took a piece and examined it thoughtfully before placing it in his pocket.

Gerston was arguing with an old man in a windbreaker. Between them stood dozens of sacks filled with bees. The old man had a portable smoker. He had gathered the bees himself.

Gerston, towering over the old man, said, "But these bees are vitally needed for research."

"They're mine," the old man protested.

Wood untied a sack and carefully peeked inside. The bees were alive. "A beekeeper?" he said.

The man nodded. "Henry David's the name, sir."

"Where's your beeyard?"

"About ten miles up the road."

"These wouldn't likely be your bees, would they? From ten miles away?"

"Who knows these days?" Henry David said. He looked dejected. "A lot of my bees have swarmed. If it keeps up, all I'll have left is the dumb ones."

"Dumb ones?" Gerston asked.

"Freak bees. No good for anything. Just collect pollen, but no honey. They're pets."

"Dumb bees," Gerston repeated.

"Anyway, with bees it's finders keepers. You know that," David wailed.

Gerston's expression said that he considered Henry David to be mentally defective, like his dumb bees. "You want to keep bees—after this?" He waved an arm.

"I don't know why the bees did it. They don't attack me like that," the man said.

"We'll buy the bees," Wood said in a tone that left no room for argument. He took out his wallet, counted some bills and handed them to the old man, who did not protest. Gerston began carrying the sacks to the station wagon. Wood looked carefully in the open sack again. Most of the bees seemed to be of normal size, but a few were giants like the one on the golf course. He said to the old man, "Take my advice. Forget about your bee-yard. Find something else to do."

PART THREE

Detrick

10

BATTLE PLAN

"I wish now to turn to a final matter," said the President of the United States, staring straight into the television camera. "As you know, a town in the great state of New York has suffered a terrible tragedy, and American hearts go out to the good people of Maryville, where twenty-four people died. Assistance is being provided by the state and federal governments already, although I know that nothing can undo the suffering that has been caused.

"Many of you have been alarmed by the appearance of these apparently hostile bees, and that is understandable. There have been rumors of dangerous bees in almost every locality in the United States. These rumors are false—I repeat, false—the product of excited imaginations. On the basis of scientific information, I report to you that the aggressive bees are localized in a few areas in our country, from which they will not be allowed to spread. Some of the finest scientists in America are now at work on the best ways and means to control and eradicate this insect.

"This they will do, rest assured. Your government is fully behind them.

"Therefore, I urge calm. I request all Americans to go about their daily lives without fear.

"Thank you and good night."

A week after Maryville, Wood collected Maria Amaral at Dulles Airport outside of Washington. Striding toward him in a black-and-white-checked pants suit and large, round dark glasses, she stood out in the stream of arriving passengers like an oil painting among watercolors. John had begun to wonder how real his feelings for Maria were. Touching her, he knew they were real—very.

"Nice trip?" he asked her.

"I hardly remember," she said, pressing close to him.

Driving to Detrick in the old Volks, John filled in the details missing from the newspaper articles. Following Maryville, Hubbard and Wood had gone to the White House and briefed the President, who had then issued a classified directive authorizing B Group to requisition whatever government facilities and equipment were required and to spend up to $25 million (a figure that would later be revised upward). B Group's existence would remain secret for the time being, to protect it from the public and the press; it was designated as a task force, operating under the U.S. Army. With great effort, Wood had been able to get a clearance for Maria, under the title Foreign Scientific Observer.

After Maryville, B Group's mood had changed from concern to alarm. Following the President's lead, the public was treating the bee invasion as a freak biological phenomenon, interesting but inconsequential. B Group felt otherwise. "The worst of it is time," John told Maria. "In June the African population will double at the least. By the end of the summer who knows how large it will be?"

"But they do not like cold. Won't they die during the winter?" Maria asked.

"I wish I knew."

At the post's entrance the Volks stopped briefly at a small red-brick guard shack that bore the words "Fort Detrick." Civilian guards, who had replaced the military police when the BW program was closed out, had been replaced by MP's once more. It was night now, but deep in the cluster of structures ahead lights blazed. "Building Five Seventy-one," Wood said cheerfully to Maria. "Here is where you'll work, eat and sleep—all with me."

"When do I start?" she said, smiling.

"You mean the work? Now, I'm afraid."

She sighed and gazed at the massive building. "What did they do here before?"

Fort Detrick, 805 acres large, lay just to the northwest of the historic town of Frederick, Maryland, where, during the Civil War, Barbara Frietchie according to a famous poem said, "Shoot, if you must, this old gray head, but spare your country's flag."

The fort had been an airport and was leased to the Maryland National Guard in 1931. Its name had been changed to "Detrick," in memory of the Guard's late flight surgeon. In 1940 Detrick was leased to the federal government to use as a pilot-training center. In 1943 it was announced that Detrick would be used by the Army's Chemical Warfare Services.

One of the best-kept American secrets of World War II was that Detrick had become the primary United States center for research and development in biological warfare.

In 1942 the National Academy of Sciences reported secretly that biological warfare was unquestionably feasible, and urged that research and development for both offensive and defensive biological warfare begin. Work started at Detrick in 1943 in a spirit of urgency. Allied intelligence indicated that the Germans and the Japanese were also investigating the possibilities of BW.

After World War II, as the Cold War accelerated, so did BW research. At the peak of its activity, in 1966, two thousand civilians were employed in the BW program. Most worked in the supersecret area behind the "inner fence" in large drab buildings that housed thousands of laboratory animals, costly experi-

115

mental gear and elaborate safety equipment. Detrick had a million-volt X-ray machine, a million-liter test sphere, or "8-ball," with walls of steel an inch and a quarter thick, for aerobiological research, electron microscopes, ultramodern research labs. A giant computer served the program.

In 1969 President Nixon announced that the United States would discontinue offensive BW research and destroy its stockpiles. In 1971 he announced that much of the old BioLab facilities would be converted to cancer research, though research on infectious diseases that might be used in wartime against the United States, or cause problems for troops, went on. The cancer program was under way, but some of the buildings, filled with equipment and miles of bare tubing, stood broodingly empty, without heat or light. One of these, four stories high, built to house animals for "8-ball" tests but completed too late to be used, was Building 571.

When Wood had finished describing Fort Detrick's past, Maria's smooth face was impassive. "But you know so much about this Fort Detrick. How is that?"

Wood hesitated, then said, "I worked here once, in the mid-nineteen-sixties, as an experimental biologist, though I really functioned as an administrator."

She stiffened. "Didn't you feel guilty about such a thing?"

He shrugged. "Not really. There seemed need of it."

"And now?"

He would only say, "Times have changed. So have I."

The fourth and third floors of the building contained the living areas; the second the lab and experimental hives; the first the bee-rearing facility; and the basement the cafeteria and command room.

The schedule for the scientific team called for a daily meeting in the command room—large, square, windowless, with bare walls, a blackboard, a lectern, a screen, a projector, a computer

116

console and a table and folding chairs. This room would be headquarters for the most complex, sophisticated war on insects ever mounted.

The scientists, all wearing long lab smocks with ID badges, gathered a little before 10 A.M., by which time they had been at work for several hours and needed a break. A uniformed soldier served coffee, and classical music came over the sound system. Today's selection was "The Flight of the Bumblebee." Wood smiled; it was one of Gerston's jokes.

At 10 sharp the music went off, and Wood opened the meeting. Present were Maria, Krim, McAllister, Gerston and Fine—all but Sheldon Hubbard, who could not be pried loose from the bee-production area overhead.

The general strategy had been developed in long meetings between various members of the group immediately after Maryville. Wood said, "All of you, except Dr. Amaral, are familiar with various aspects of the plan; now you will see it in its entirety. The important thing is to coordinate our efforts so as to insure that information each of you has will reach others among you who may need it."

Wood paused as though to underscore the point. Slides had been prepared. He dimmed the lights with the rheostat on the wall and went to the projector. The first slide flashed on the screen.

COMMUNICATION INTERFERENCE

SUBVERSION

MIND CONTROL

PHYSICAL ATTACK

CHEMICAL WARFARE

GENETIC WARFARE

"Note," Wood went on, "that what is outlined here corresponds to modern warfare in its most advanced form. We will

117

attack the enemy on every level, from his reproductive system to his adult life and the very genes he carries." He pressed a button, and another slide appeared.

Five-Stage Plan

PHASE ONE: "BEE" COCKTAIL
PHASE TWO: PROJECT QUEEN
PHASE THREE: PROJECT BRUSH FIRE
PHASE FOUR: PROJECT STERILE MALE
PHASE FIVE: DESTRUCTION
PHASE SIX: URBAN DEFENSES

Wood said, "Each phase of the operation will reduce the enemy in numbers and strength. By the fifth phase the enemy ought to be weakened to the point where he can be picked off, more or less hive by hive. It would be useless to go out in the woods and try this now—the enemy is simply too strong. There are too many of him." He glanced at the outline. "The beauty of the plan is that it avoids mass use of pesticides."

He pressed the button again, and the screen said:

BEE COCKTAIL

AMERICAN FOULBROOD
INSECT GROWTH REGULATOR (IGR)
ANTIPHEROMONE SUBSTANCE

Wood continued: "This will be the first weapon deployed, in mid-May. Thousands of packets containing these substances in honey solution will be dropped over infested areas. They should kill some of the larvae, interfere with the development of others, and mess up the bees' communications system. I'll make the cocktail my responsibility."

McAllister's high-pitched voice interrupted. "Hold it. You mean to drop AFB? I didn't know that. What about the apiaries? You'll infect them too."

"No. Beekeepers will be notified to start giving their bees Terramycin and sulfathiozole early."

"The honey will be unfit to eat."

Wood drawled, "Well, there won't be any honey from these areas."

McAllister said stubbornly, "The other ingredients in the cocktail may get into the domestic hives as well."

"We'll be dropping in the forests. If worse comes to worst, and we do kill off domestic bees in some areas, then we must. New York, say, will be without apples for a year, because there won't be any pollination. The trees will survive."

McAllister groaned. Wood changed the slide.

PROJECT QUEEN

LINE-REARING QUEENS
NEGATIVE SURVIVAL CHARACTERISTICS

Wood said, "The queens will be the first factory-bred bees to emerge. Like the others, hundreds of millions will be dropped by helicopters over the infested areas. They will mate with the Africans, enter the hives and do battle with the African queens. Some must prevail for the scheme to work. The idea is that they will pass on defects to their progeny, and that their queens and drones will similarly breed and increase the defective population until enough Africans have enough bad genes to make them self-destructive."

Negative survival characteristics involved genetic surgery. That was Krim's department, and the short young geneticist was shaking his beard. Colonies of defective bees were about to be flown from the experimental apiary at the University of California at Davis. They had droopy wings and flew poorly. It was plain that Krim had doubts about feasibility.

Wood showed another slide.

PROJECT BRUSH FIRE

LINE-BEARING WORKERS
STIMULATE AGGRESSION

"We'll drop factory-reared workers—hundreds of millions of them—keyed up with the attack pheromone. They will be our foot soldiers. They will be chemically compelled to search for and attack any beehive in the vicinity. If they do their job, they ought to reduce the African population," Wood explained. "This will be McAllister's area."

PROJECT STERILE MALE

LINE-BEARING DRONES
STERILIZATION

"Gerston's baby," Wood said. Hundreds of millions of drones would be mass-produced at the facility and sterilized. They, too, would be dropped from the air. Mating with African queens, they would insert useless sperm in them. The queens, when filled, would not mate again, but would be unfertilized, and would thus lay only drone eggs.

"That's it. In something like this you have to try everything you can and hope some of it works. In my opinion, any one of these control techniques should do the job. Then trained bee wardens will enter the forests and finish them off. It's pretty neat, if you ask me."

Fine had been taking notes. He glanced at them. "You've

only gone to Phase Five. If the wild bees are as good as dead, why do we need Phase Six—'Urban Defenses'?"

"There's always the chance the bees will get through. You have to consider it," Wood answered.

"And attack the central cities?" Fine asked. He looked appalled.

"A chance, yes," Wood said slowly.

11

SPREAD

The following morning the same group assembled again. Maria Amaral had been up almost all night working with the Detrick computer via the console. Behind the glasses her dark eyes looked tired.

Using data about bee incidents gathered by Fine's allergists, who had been rechecking suspicious deaths, the computer had made certain assumptions about the density of the Africanized bee population throughout the United States. Because deaths from bee stings had been more or less uniform until three years before, it was assumed that the giant mutants, the toxic bees, had first emerged at that time, though undoubtedly in small numbers. A careful review of suspicious case histories, even an exhumation of bodies in some cases, proved conclusively that many deaths attributed to heart attacks, organophosphate poisoning or even standard anaphylactic shock had in fact been caused by the strange African sting. Deaths from bee stings had been increasing at a rapid rate since, but more in some areas than others. A computerized map of the United States was flashed on the screen.

Maria tapped the map with a pointer. The scientists still tended to concentrate on her rather than on what she was saying, a fact that infuriated Wood. She tapped again. "The total number of incidents that we now attribute to African bees is nearly one thousand. Such incidents have occurred in many places. Isolated instances are marked with X's." She moved the pointer to the shaded places. "But the preponderance of incidents has occurred in three areas, which would indicate that the Africans are concentrated there. As you can see, these areas are in the northwest, north-central and northeast parts of the country."

Maria took a sip of water. Wood knew she was under great strain. A miscalculation made by the computer on the basis of faulty material she had given it could be costly. "You will note that the main movement of the bees appears to be north to south, based on the casualty patterns."

"Is there any way to calculate the speed of spread?" Wood asked.

"It is only a guess. The computer estimates the main body is presently spreading out at a rate of perhaps a hundred miles a year."

"That's slower than they've moved in Brazil," McAllister objected.

Amaral answered, "The rate of advance may change as the population builds."

"When does the computer bring the bees into a major city?" Wood asked.

Amaral pressed some keys on the console. The map faded and the screen said:

PROJECTED ARRIVAL DATES
AFRICANIZED BEES
NEW YORK TWO YEARS PLUS
CHICAGO TWO YEARS PLUS
SAN FRANCISCO TWO YEARS PLUS

Wood said quickly, "Of course, the defense scheme hasn't been built into the computer's predictions."

"No. Of course not," Amaral said.

123

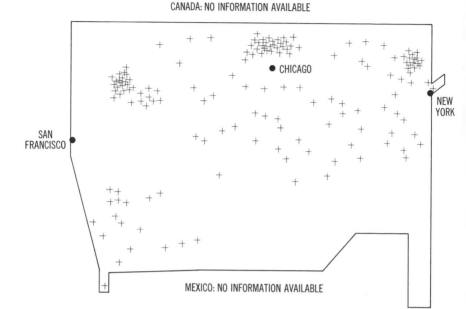

Fig. II: Computer map, May 1. Crosses (+) mark isolated bee incidents. Shaded areas represent major concentrations of hostile bees. (Courtesy Apicultural Research and Development Facility, Fort Detrick, Maryland)

The "S" in "PLUS" continued to flash until Maria gave the machine more instructions, and the map returned.

Nobody spoke for a moment, and then McAllister piped, "It's a singular thing. It's all wrong."

Wood felt dazed. "It is. I had always assumed there were two possible avenues of invasion—by ship and over the Mexican border. But the ship theory, slim as it was, doesn't account for the concentration in the Midwest, unless we assume the bees came in through the St. Lawrence Seaway. From the look of it, there aren't enough hostile bees in Texas to support the idea of a border crossing in force."

They stared at the map, and then Maria said, "It isn't as it is in Brazil either. In my country the bees spread fastest to the tropical parts. But there are no incidents in your South at all. You'd expect Africans in the South."

Wood said, "Yes, it's puzzling. It's north to south, all right."

"But where did these bees come from? What are they?" Maria cried.

An idea began to grow in Wood's mind. "Could they have traveled *after* they were in the United States?"

McAllister reached the right conclusion first. He snapped his fingers. "The U.S. mail. It's plain as day. The breeders."

Wood said, "Yes, that's got to be it. African bees are being bred in the South and shipped north and west to beekeepers to replace their stocks. And that breeder or breeders imported them."

A single tube of bee semen would have been enough.

Or a nucleus of bees—a queen, a few drones, a cupful of workers—a package small enough to slip into a paper bag or even a pocket.

Or a little parcel of drones. A cigarette case with air holes cut in it would have sufficed.

Or a piece of comb, with a queen, workers and brood cells.

In 1922 the United States had prohibited the import of foreign bees because they were bringing with them a tiny eight-legged tick called the Acarine mite. But it was perfectly legal to import bee brood or semen. USDA discouraged the practice in the case of Africans; still, some greedy breeder, in Brazil for a conference or a buying trip, realizing that the new bees in Brazil were superb producers of honey, could have bought African bees from a Brazilian bee man who himself doubted the true nature of *adansonii*. If he had purchased semen, it would have been even easier.

In a single morning an experienced bee man could squeeze a hundred or so drones and collect their sperm in a test tube. A

125

small quantity would fertilize any number of queens. A queen is anesthetized with carbon dioxide, then she is clamped on a small rack, and semen is inserted into her vagina with a small syringe.

"There are a few breeders who know how to do that," McAllister observed. "One large breeder might have been enough. He could produce thousands of queens with African blood and ship them north. He might keep some African stock on hand for rebreeding, so he goes right on producing and shipping hybrid African queens."

Wood asked, "But why didn't the northern beekeepers who got the Africanized bees have trouble with their offspring? They haven't reported any."

Krim rose to his full five-foot-five and began to pace. He said in his slurred, seemingly arrogant fashion, "We shouldn't use the word 'breeder.' Not enough is known about bee genetics to breed them; we know a lot more about breeding horses. 'Rearer' is more exact. The bee rearer has a queen who herself is a hybrid of Africanized Brazilian bees. She's a half-breed. She mates. Her offspring may be only one-quarter African. They are also a minority in a temperate climate. All three factors could operate in making the African's violent nature disappear temporarily. But don't forget that the African strain is dominant. All experience shows us that."

"For me that still doesn't quite clarify the long status quo in northern beeyards," Wood said.

"Maybe they have to reach certain levels in the population before they assert themselves," Gerston commented.

Maria said, "It is true that in Brazil small colonies are not so excitable. Further, these Africans have a tendency to abscond when the population grows. When a hive becomes African, it moves out to the jungle."

McAllister waved his hands. "The Africans don't cluster like our bees. They wouldn't make it through winter."

"*Pure* Africans," Krim corrected him sourly. "These bees also have the genetic information of American bees."

From the pocket of his lab smock Wood took a plastic box. In it was the hive lining, or propolis, taken from the tree at Maryville. "The sample has been carefully analyzed, and there's no doubt about it. These bees have developed the capability to use Styrofoam in their building materials. It's simple to work with, and it must improve their insulation enormously. It might make wintering simple."

Krim said, "That confirms it. The purer Africans, and their next evolutionary phase, the giants, would appear first in the wilds. There they'd build up rapidly. Natural breeding habits would make the wild drones mate with the hive queens, so you'd be Africanizing or re-Africanizing the American hives, though more slowly. At some point all bees, whether wild or in hives, would turn African. I don't know when that point is."

Wood said, "All right. But what about that beekeeper in the South? He's raising queens, and queens don't sting, so he wouldn't notice anything unusual. But what about the queen's worker progeny? Wouldn't he notice their aggressiveness?"

"Breeders keep stock in small colonies," McAllister pointed out.

"And even the southern United States is more temperate than tropical Brazil," Amaral said in her low, urgent voice. "That would pacify them, too, until they acclimatized."

"But his queens are crossbreeding with their own drones. Their progeny would also be getting more African all the time," Krim said.

"And therefore more dangerous. We ought to find this southern breeder at once—but how? There must be hundreds of them," Wood said.

Gerston remarked, "He's probably in an isolated area to protect his hive from other lines. And if his bees did turn aggressive, he'd probably want to suppress the news. But I think we'll get wind of him."

"Where?" Wood said.

"From the local coroner." Gerston's expression said, *And he deserves it.*

12

THE BEE FACTORY

Though Maria had been on the premises over thirty-six hours, she had not had time to look around. When the meeting ended, Wood said to her, "Hubbard wants to give you a guided tour. I better warn you—is he proud of his bee factory!"

Its official name was Apicultural Research and Development Facility, but the scientists called it the "bee factory." With construction under way, lights blazed all night, bringing questions but no answers from Detrick, whose inner fence was as tightly sealed as during bacteriological-warfare days. But some foreign governments had been told the truth to avoid suspicion that American BW research had been reactivated. These governments began to watch the American experiment closely.

There was no time to devise new equipment. Rather, the techniques had to grow out of previously existing technology and knowledge of insects, especially knowledge about the most studied insect of all, the honeybee.

After his embarrassment at having planned a factory that would have to be at least eight miles long, Hubbard had redesigned it, with charts on bee development before him and a team of architects and engineers at his side. For the zoologist, the facility had to meet several criteria. It had to be quick to assemble, therefore using easily available equipment. Above all it had to function effectively from the beginning. To correct

129

mistakes and start over could make the effort too late to help.

"I believe that his first and fundamentally most important decision," Wood told a reporter some time later, "was to avoid automation here. Things that we might have been able to do with machinery we did by hand. It enabled us to get into production at the start of May."

They found Hubbard on the factory floor above, supervising the installation of a long line of large incubators. Waving, he flew over, his lab coat flapping and the two antennalike projections of his hair standing straight up. To Wood, Hubbard had never looked happier.

"Welcome!" he boomed. "Come to have a peep at my lair? Don't get many visitors, you know." Without waiting for an answer, he took Maria's arm and led her along, with Wood trailing behind. "Well, I am the last person in the world to use hyperbole like 'miracle.' I certainly won't claim that what we are about to accomplish here is a miracle. I will only say that nobody, *nobody*, has succeeded in doing anything remotely like it. We are going to assembly-line-rear bees. What's more, we will manufacture a billion of them a month."

"A *billion?*" Maria cried, winking at Wood. "But how is that possible?"

Hubbard chuckled. "I'll show you. At this minute you are in the middle of a giant beehive."

Maria twisted her head, and Wood's eyes followed hers. Around them were incubators, glass panels, metal carts, tubing, piles of plastic boxes and plastic squares. "*A beehive?*" she said.

"Come over here."

They entered a large area bathed in yellow light, separated into three sections by glass partitions. In each were long rows of shelves, ten feet high, containing small wire cages. "This is the laying area," Hubbard explained. "Each of the three sections is

130

color-designated—blue for queens, white for drones, brown for workers. Got that?"

"Blue for queens, white for drones, brown for workers," Maria repeated dutifully.

Hubbard said with visible excitement, "We are in the process of procuring queens from southern breeders. They will arrive in a few days, about twenty thousand of them. We don't expect all our queens to survive or prove out as egg-layers, but we need only about sixteen thousand laying queens to meet our daily quota of eggs."

"Will the queens have already been fertilized?" she wanted to know.

"Some—by the breeders—but not all. There isn't time. The virgin queens arriving here will be fertilized by artificial insemination. Look."

Hubbard led them to a large chamber filled with banks of work tables holding rows of small machines. These devices would be used for the artificial insemination of queens, the zoologist explained.

"Then what happens?"

"The queens will be permitted to produce one kind of bee only—either workers, drones, or other queens. The laying queens will have no choice in the matter."

Hubbard picked up one of the wire cages and removed from it a piece of plastic somewhat less than a foot square. The plastic was covered with hundreds of tiny indentations. He said, "Any plastics manufacturer can turn out these platens by the millions. The indentations correspond to the brood cells on a comb." He left them briefly and returned with two more platens. "See, the indentations are of different sizes. The largest ones are queen cells, the smallest worker cells. The queen drops her eggs into these cells. The eggs are precisely the same. The ones dropped in the large cells become queens, the ones left in the small cells

131

become workers. Our queens are divided into three groups. Each gets one kind of platen to lay on." He glanced at the platen with medium-size cells. "Ah, but do you understand how a queen produces drones?"

"Not exactly," Maria confessed, showing even, white teeth. Wood smiled too.

Hubbard, clearly delighted, explained. "Well, once a queen has mated, she carries in her body all the sperm she needs for life. There are so many surprising things about bees, but none more so, for my money, than the fact that the queen chooses, in some fashion we don't understand, to fertilize some eggs with sperm but not others. The eggs she leaves unfertilized become drones. We will leave some queens deliberately unfertilized. The unfertilized queens will lay drone eggs in the medium-size cells."

Maria inspected the platen. "But there are so many cells. How long does it take a queen to fill them?"

"Each platen," Hubbard said, "contains about two thousand cells, which corresponds to the queen's daily laying capacity. All day she crawls over the platen filling up the cells. Each day the platen is removed from this covered slot and a new one is inserted."

Maria shook her head. "I have so many questions. Who feeds the queens?"

"Each queen will be accompanied by a group of workers. The workers feed from tubes of sugar-water and a pollen substitute stuck in the sides of the cages. Then the workers feed the laying queens."

"Why is it so hot in here?"

"The temperature—which is ninety-six degrees Fahrenheit—and the relative humidity—seventy percent—correspond exactly to hive conditions. We're testing the equipment at the moment. Come outside."

Outside the laying area it was cool again. Hubbard pointed

back. "Now, as you saw, there are three laying areas. In the worker, or brown, area all the platens have the small cells. In the drone, or white, area all the cells are drone-size, and in the queen, or blue, section all the platens have the large cells."

Maria shook her head in confusion, and Hubbard grinned. Finally Maria said, "So a queen becomes a queen solely by virtue of brood-cell size?"

Hubbard answered, "No." He pointed to three rows of massive incubators, each row separate and painted white, blue, or brown. These incubators, which already existed at Detrick, were square ten-foot boxes, containing 1,000 cubic feet of space. Hubbard explained that each could comfortably hold 1,200 platens on racks from floor to ceiling. Each would hold 2,400,000 eggs. There were less than 100 incubators in all.

"Wheeled on the carts to the properly color-coded incubators," Hubbard continued, "the eggs enter the larval phase. Now they must be fed. On the floor above are vats which have been set up to feed nutrients down through tubes to the incubators, which contain nebulizers, or diffusion devices, which spread the nutrient evenly, so that it settles into the larval cells. Now, to answer your question, all larvae get the queen substance, royal jelly, for three days. Then the workers and drones get a high-protein nutrient called beebread, but the queens go on receiving royal jelly for three more days. The rich diet seems to be what makes queens out of them; the larger cell size is merely to accommodate their bodies. The food we serve here will be synthetic, of course." Shelly Hubbard rubbed his hands.

"It is certainly ingenious," Maria said encouragingly. "What happens next?"

"Well, on the ninth day after the egg is laid, in the case of queens and workers, and the eleventh for the drones, the larvae pupate. In the hive the cell is sealed, but it has been discovered that if temperature and humidity are ideal, an exterior covering

133

will suffice. When the larvae are ready to pupate, the platens are placed in lightweight plastic boxes, three platens, or six thousand bees, to a box, in a color-coded storage area." He pointed to the dim recesses of the building. "When the bees reach pupation they will be stored, and then dropped on the enemy. It'll work; there is no doubt that we can actually produce a billion bees a month. But these won't be your normal civilian bees. *My* bees will be soldiers, bred to fight."

Wood spoke for the first time. "And win, we hope."

After John and Maria had left, Hubbard started an animated conversation with an insect-growth specialist about the possibility of using a chemical combination to speed up the development of the factory-created bees. Suddenly Gerston ran up.

Gerston had been on the phone all morning supervising the purchase of the last of the twenty thousand queens. Such a number was well within the capability of the breeders, but it did mean depleting their stocks and hurting their production capacity. Some were reluctant to sell, but when necessary Gerston twisted arms.

He had been querying breeders about their stocks—he did not want to buy Africans by accident.

"I found one," he said to Hubbard.

"Found what?" the beetle asked sharply. He did not like to be interrupted.

"A tribe of Mau Maus. In Florida."

Hubbard understood at once. "What about the breeder?" he asked. "'He must have been the one to start all this."

"That's how I located the Mau Maus. The breeder and his family were just found dead."

The scene was not hard to imagine—official vehicles screaming down a Florida highway. Evacuation of the area. Gas masks, cyanide guns. There would be countless such skirmishes before the battle began.

13

TOXICITY

George Fine was tired. He had been working since 6 A.M. in the experimental hive, and as if the problems confronting him were not already complicated enough, there had been a row with Sheldon Hubbard.

He could see Hubbard now through the glass partitions, his two wings of dark hair standing straight up. The zoologist, in his white lab coat, seemed to be everywhere at once as he drove the bee factory to completion. His energy was inexhaustible. George Fine envied him that.

The experimental hive and the lab area were located on the second floor of the building. All interior structures built for the facility were glass, and so were the hives, which were equipped with Detrick safety features. It had been done rapidly—too rapidly, in Fine's opinion. Meticulous as always, he had gone over the hive complex almost bolt by bolt, investigating every feature. He thought the doors to the chambers where the bees were kept opened the wrong way—in. He even objected to the handles and catches, which appeared flimsy to him. In his haste to get rolling, Hubbard had cut corners.

Fine had trouble getting Hubbard to slow down long enough to hear him out. Finally he was able to explain his position. Hubbard, deep-set eyes glowering with annoyance, replied that Detrick had always used inward-opening doors for its animal labs. As for the handles, he did not expect the bees to be using

135

them, he said. Stiff with humiliation, Fine went back to his experiment.

He had never worked with bees, but the techniques he would need were relatively simple and easy to master.* The bees brought from Maryville had been subdued with carbon dioxide and separated into two categories—the Afro-Americans and the giant mutant bees. Building 571 was attached to the million-liter test sphere once used at Detrick for aerosol testing. The hive area had been built adjacent to the 8-ball, with connecting passages, so that the bees could fly through ports into the sphere itself, which became their flying area. The bees, by instinct, would always return to the same hives.

The bees occupied room-sized chambers in which standard wood Langstroth hives had been placed, with combs filled with honey, and pollen hung on the back walls, which opened into the flying area. There were flowers in large pots to simulate a natural environment.

Fine now donned a personnel safety suit that had been used in experimental research at Detrick. It was all in one piece, made of soft translucent plastic, except for the clear-plastic window in the head-hood portion which could be opened. Only one change had been made from the original design, and that because of B Group's decision to use cyanide in the event that bees got into the pass-through chambers. The suit had been provided with a backpack oxygen canister. The canister not only provided air for breathing but also maintained a positive air pressure within the suit, thus protecting the wearer if cyanide was released in the chamber.

This suit also had another important advantage. The bee that had stung Wood through a light leather glove had taught B Group that ordinary clothing was not adequate protection. The

---

* One article read by George Fine was Albert F. Gunnison, "An Improved Method for Collecting the Liquid Fraction of Bee Venom," *Journal of Apicultural Research*, 5 (1) :33–36 (1966).

surface of the plastic suit was too smooth for a bee sting to lodge in.

Fine stepped into the pass-through airlock, which looked like a shower stall, carefully shutting the outer door behind him. He then reopened the inner door and entered the chamber of the giant bees. The routine would be the same on leaving; if bees got into the airlock, it could be flooded with cyanide by pressing a button. The safety procedure took seconds, and guaranteed that no bees would escape.

Fine carried with him an oblong box, about three feet long and a foot wide, covered with a grid of steel wires over a polyethylene sheet. A cord extended from the box. Fine plugged the cord into a socket and then pressed a switch. The wires were charged with exactly three volts at a frequency of fifteen cycles per second.

A large black bee with orange markings emerged from the hive, hovered over the box, and lit on the wires, which shocked. The bee immediately stung the wires and flew away. A second bee did the same. By the time a half dozen bees had stung the wires the bees' alarm-defense pheromone had been set off to the hive; the odor, contained in the sting, conveyed the presence of an enemy. Now the bee horde streamed out in earnest.

Fine, standing ignored in the corner, was treated to a breathtaking display of African fury. Again and again the aroused Africans attacked with their barbs, lowering their abdomens and stabbing the wires. The war chant, *ziiiiiiii*, filled the chamber.

At last Fine turned off the gadget. The exhausted bees returned to the hive. Not one followed him into the chamber.

Having removed his safety suit, Fine studied the polyethylene sheet. The stings had passed between the wires and penetrated the thin sheet, leaving some barbs, but not nearly as many as Fine expected. Probably five thousand bees had stung the polyethylene, but no more than a hundred had lost their stings —itself a commentary on the exceptional strength of the giants which would live to sting again. The venom, coating the underside of the sheet, was a brown, viscous liquid that gave off a dry, bananalike odor—the smell of the alarm pheromone in the sting. Volatile, it dried in a few minutes, and Fine carefully scraped the brown, gummy residue into a glass vial.

He then began a long chemical analysis. First, the venom went into a centrifuge, which separated out any contaminating foreign matter, such as stingers or bits of wing material. Next came infrared analysis, which provided a crude chemical profile. Finally, and most important, Fine used the computerized gas-chromatograph, mass-spectrometer system. A benzene solution of the venom was injected into the instrument, which then

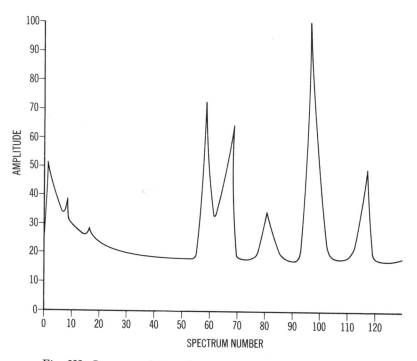

Fig. III: Spectographic analysis—toxic bee venom (Courtesy estate of Dr. George Fine)

138

separated the venom components and analyzed each by molecular fragmentation. The results appeared as a tracing, and Fine saw a clear difference from standard bee venom. Standard bee venom had seven peaks—this tracing had eight.

It was this eighth substance that interested George Fine. He queried the computerized instrument for more information on its nature. The machine was quiet for a second, and then the printout began. The computer printed its prompts in capital letters, and Fine responded with his directions and inquiries in numbers and lower-case letters.

```
OPERATION MODE:   ms print
FILE NAME:   mg5–4
SCAN:   403
BACKGROUND FILE:   mg5–4
SCAN:
```

Fine paused, re-examined the tracing, and then responded with "65." The computer went on.

```
MULTIPLIER:
BASE PEAK:
```

Because he had taken a standard default option, Fine ignored these prompts and waited.

```
LOWER THRESHOLD PERCENT:  0.05
```

With the parameters set, Fine was ready. He pushed two keys on the instrument, which began to hum and chatter. The recorder and its mechanical pen produced a bar graph of peaks associated with the unknown eighth substance; then the printer typed out a listing of all the numerical values associated with the peaks.

The toxicologist had no way of knowing what substance the

bar graph and all the numerical values described. For that he would have to rely on another computer, a much larger one. Taking all the information with him, Fine walked down two flights of metal steps to the basement command room. It was late and the windowless chamber was empty. The console there was linked not only with the Detrick computer but also, by telephone terminal, with an even larger one at the National Institutes of Health near Washington which keeps on its reels a central chemical-compound data bank—the most complete in the world.

Fine dialed a phone number that served to link the console with the NIH computer. The machine became activated, saying:

SCIENCE IS DEAD LONG LIVE THE COMPUTER

Fine swore. Late at night, in the cheerless command room, he had no stomach for the silly jokes programmers insisted on feeding the machines.

The computer then listed by name and number the functions it could perform. There were sixteen of them.

The machine paused, humming quietly while awaiting Fine's instructions. The toxicologist thought a moment and then typed back "5."

The machine said:

NHLI MASS SPECTRAL SEARCH SYSTEM
PROGRAM: YOUR NAME AND COMPANY PLEASE
USER:

Fine said:

Apicultural Research and Development Facility, Ft. Detrick, Maryland
PROGRAM: PLEASE TYPE YOUR 3 INITIALS
USER:

140

It so happened that George Fine did not have a middle name. He typed "gf."

The machine repeated on the printout:

PROGRAM: PLEASE TYPE YOUR 3 INITIALS
USER:

Again Fine cursed. If he did not give himself a middle initial the machine would refuse to proceed. He typed "gnf."

Satisfied, the machine said:

PROGRAM: TO SEARCH FOR PEAKS, TYPE PEAKS
TO SEARCH FOR MOLECULAR WEIGHT, TYPE MW
TO SEARCH FOR PEAKS WITH MF, TYPE PMF
TO SEARCH FOR MOLECULAR FORMULA, TYPE MY
TO PRINT OUT PEAKS/INTENSITIES, TYPE SPEC
TO PERFORM A SIMILARITY COMPARISON, TYPE SIM
TO PLOT SPECTRA ON DISPLAY TERMINAL, TYPE PLOT
TO LIST THE MSDC CODES, TYPE LIST
TO EXIT FROM THE PROGRAM, TYPE OUT
USER:

Fine paused, though only momentarily, and then typed "peaks."
The machine responded:

PROGRAM: MASS SPEC PEAK AND INTENSITY
SEARCH
USER: INTENSITY RANGE FACTOR FOR THIS
SEARCH IS?

Fine answered "3." The computer gave additional instructions for the search input:

CR TO EXIT, 1 FOR ID #/NAMES OR FOR ID, MW,
MF AND NAME
USER:

Fine turned to the foot-long sheet of yellow paper containing the printout of numerical values for the unknown eighth substance. He scanned it rapidly and then typed "219, 100." The search was on.

PROGRAM: FOUND 296 SPECTRA WITH M/E PEAK: 219
USER: 108, 25
PROGRAM: FOUND 150 SPECTRA WITH M/E PEAK: 108
USER: 77, 22
PROGRAM: FOUND 24 SPECTRA WITH M/E PEAK: 77

Carrying on a dialogue with the computer in this way, Fine gradually narrowed the range of possibilities. Then, as the computer came back with its routinely prompt "USER," Fine responded with "231, 19," and the machine balked.

PROGRAM: THERE ARE NO SPECTRA IN THE OPEN
FILE WITH THAT COMBINATION OF M/E PEAKS
AND INTENSITIES DISREGARD PEAK OF 231 AND
CONTINUE (CON) OR EXIT (OUT)?
USER:

It seemed useless to continue with the open file, but Fine had no intention of exiting. Without hesitation he typed:
override. access closed file.

The computer reacted immediately.

password.

For the third time since he began the search Fine swore. Damn passwords, damn secrecy. His irritation receded as abruptly as it flared. No sooner had the computer typed "PASS-WORD" than it automatically began preparations to Fine's response.

First it typed five double-spaced X's:

X X X X X

Then it typed five double-spaced O's directly over the X's:

142

Ⓧ Ⓧ Ⓧ Ⓧ Ⓧ

It repeated the process with a number of other characters, until the five areas looked almost like solid black squares:

▇ ▇ ▇ ▇ ▇

Now it was ready for Fine to type the password. Typed on those black areas, the individual characters of the password would not be visually recognizable. But the electronic message they transmitted to the computer when he typed them would gain him access to the closed file. He typed B Group's password, "kilbe," over the five black squares.

The computer replied almost immediately:

```
PROGRAM: FOUND ONE SPECTRA WITH M/E PEAK: 98
REF M/E PEAKS 219 108 77 231
USER: GIVE ID AND NAME
PROGRAM: DESIGNATION CLASSIFIED. FOUND IN
FILE UNDER FILE ZP-1096A. EDGEWOOD ARSENAL, MD.
USER:
```

Fine sat back, flabbergasted. The information could mean only one thing. Edgewood Arsenal is to chemical warfare what Detrick had been to BW. The substance that the deadly toxic fraction in the bee sting resembled more closely than any known substance in the world was an agent developed for chemical warfare.

It was now 11 P.M. on Saturday evening, too late to contact Edgewood. George Fine, sitting in the bare-walled room, was suddenly depressed. The news he had received was frightening—so much so, that he decided not to tell the others until he had the facts. He was also lonely. His only real exchanges of the day had been with machines, and he longed for his wife, who had died a little over two years before. Wearily, Fine turned to the keyboard and typed his response to the computer's last prompting:

out

He left before the tireless machine finished informing him how much time and money he had spent.

14

ETHOGRAM

Sunday. Same place. Same lab smocks (clean in the morning). Though more tired, same faces—except for Sheldon Hubbard's. He could not be torn from the bee factory.

Gerston burst in with *The Washington Post*. Wood glanced at the headline. "My God!" he said. They crowded around.

AFRO BEES STING CITRUS TOWN
42 Dead, 37 Wounded

GROVEVILLE, Fla. (AP)—African honeybees today devastated this peaceful town, with 42 persons dead and 37 wounded.

Of the dead, 23 were elementary-school children.

Near Groveville is a large plant for making canned orange juice. Orange rinds, waiting to be incinerated, appear to have originally attracted the large bee swarm.

When the bees were sighted the plant was closed at once, and workers fled the scene in their cars.

One worker, William Masters, 35, was stung to death, however, when he came too close to the bees. His brother Robert, 45, also worked at the plant. Apparently crazed with grief, Robert Masters climbed into a bulldozer and drove it into the mound of orange pulp. Robert Masters was also stung to death.

State Department of Agriculture personnel, armed with cyanide equipment, had already been summoned. When they arrived, the bees had already abandoned the scene. Authorities speculate that their hive was or is in nearby swampland. But instead of returning there, the bees, buzzing loudly, wheeled toward the town of Groveville.

They concentrated their attack on an elementary school that was being used for a Little League baseball game.

Children in the playground were attacked first. The survivors ran inside. Adults closed doors and windows.

The school is fully air-conditioned for summer use, but the system was being repaired. An intake vent was open. Into this vent the bees poured, emerging in the classroom through the air-conditioning ducts.

The results were frightful. The children and parents used the only weapons they had at hand—school books—to no avail.

The surviving bees then departed.

One previous mass attack by the deadly African bees has been reported in Florida.

Authorities fear there may be more.

A single funeral for all the dead is to take place on Wednesday.

The reports from the allergists and from Fort Detrick's radio room, which also had news-wire teletypes, were fed directly into the computer, which then summarized them. Maria pressed a button and the screen lit up. In south-central Florida, a cold and precise X had appeared, devoid of human drama and tragedy.

It was not far from another X—representing the bee breeder and his family.

"So they didn't kill all the Florida swarm after all," Wood said slowly.

"I guess we should be reading the papers," Gerston said. "You don't get much of a story from the computer map."

"No, we *shouldn't* be reading the papers," Wood said forcefully. "We have a mission and shouldn't be distracted from it. The map is all the news we need." He looked at the headline again, shook his head and murmured, "God." Then he turned to Fine and asked what the toxicologist had learned about the African venom.

Fine said, "A venom is a complex mixture of substances capable of producing a variety of physical and pharmacological changes. It is neurotoxic, that is, it disturbs the nervous system and also hemolizes the red cells. The two fractions in normal bee venom responsible for most of the trouble are phospholipasa A., which can cause respiratory paralysis, and hyaluronidase, a surface-active substance which increases tissue permeability so that the venom is spread in the body of the host who receives it. Both these fractions are found in cobra venom. Am I going too fast?"

They sat up. Fine took a sip of coffee and continued. "The reason a bee isn't as dangerous as a cobra is that the bee has less venom to deliver. It's just that simple."

Gerston said, "The big bees have larger venom sacs. They want to be cobras."

"No, I don't think so," Fine replied. "The African is still a bee. By itself, the venom of a giant bee would hurt like hell but it wouldn't normally kill. This bee has done something else. It has managed to combine phospholipasa A. with another chemical into a new fraction—I'm still trying to find out what it is, but it has something to do with organophosphates, I'm sure."

Wood said somberly, "How did the African get on to that trick?" He looked at Gerston.

"It's like the Vietnam 'hoppers." the tall entomologist said. "The bee got exposed to a pesticide and learned to metabolize it."

"And once they can do that, you know it's a genetic trait," Krim observed.

Fine objected, "But not all Africans are toxic. I've established that. Only the giants are."

They took this in. Krim said, as though thinking out loud, "But all Africans are mutating toward giganticism. And when they become giants they have the toxic capability. Is toxicity a function of size?"

Gerston answered, "But not a cause necessarily. It may be

that they have developed the appetite for organophosphates—if that's what we're talking about—but can't metabolize the stuff until they get bigger. Then they ingest it, as the grasshoppers do. There's plenty of it around, God knows."

"But how did they learn such a thing?" Fine wondered.

Maria said, "In Brazil farmers have been attacking the Africans for years with DDT and organophosphates."

"And they learned about pesticides," Gerston said.

Krim cut them down. "Please don't talk about 'learning.' I don't believe rapid adaptations or mutations—call them what you like—could have been learned. Is it really possible that a fly could adapt itself in a couple of generations to being resistant to DDT? No. Somehow the insects have been preprogrammed. They carry potential mutations for a variety of conditions, many of which probably don't even exist yet. It's as though a broad range of contingencies had already been planned for. Insects seem to immediately develop a survival mechanism for every change in the environment."

Wood said musingly, "Faced with natural enemies, the African bee got vicious. Confronted with cold, it used plastic."

"Perhaps its size helps the giant attack and overpower smaller bees," Krim said quickly.

Wood stared at him. After an uncomfortable silence he said, "But they haven't grown larger anywhere else, only here. To me that says that here the odds for them are worse. Life is harder. Maybe smaller bees succumb more easily to the colder climate. Maybe the presence of strong hives requires big bees to overcome them. Clearly, the Africans are getting larger because they need to. But exactly what the advantage is to them we're still not sure. Let's look at the ethogram. Are you ready, Mac?"

For the past week in the 8-ball and experimental hives, McAllister had been conducting tests on the captive bees from Maryville to establish their capabilities. As an experienced bee man, he said boastfully, he had no fear of bees, African or any other kind. He had tried working some of the smaller Africans with his bare fingers, and the painful result was concealed under gauze and adhesive tape. McAllister's folly led to a rule laid down by Wood: No one could enter the experimental hives without an observer present to sound the alarm.

McAllister's results had been fed to the computer, which collated and recorded them, shaping them into a biological profile, or ethogram—a catalogue of behavioral characteristics.* On the screen words appeared.

```
ETHOGRAM FOLLOWS
APIS MELLIFERA
ADANSONII MARYVILLIS
"N" DESIGNATES "NORMAL"
"NORMAL" DESIGNATES NO
DIFFERENCE FROM
EUROBEE CHARACTERISTICS
"EUROBEE" DESIGNATES
EUROPEAN-AMERICAN
BEE
ADANSONII MARYVILLIS
ETHOGRAM FOLLOWS
```

The words faded and new ones appeared.

```
BODY LENGTH
QUEEN 2 INCHES
DRONE 1½ INCHES
WORKER 1 INCH
VISUAL ACUITY
DAY (N)
NIGHT (HIGH)
SOUND PERCEPTION (N)
GRAVITY PERCEPTION (N)
TASTE PERCEPTION (HIGH)
```

* McAllister adapted the ethogram from Edward O. Wilson, *The Insect Societies* (Cambridge, Mass.: Belknap Press of Harvard University Press, 1971).

```
WAGGLE DANCE (N)
HIVE POPULATION 75,000–100,000
LEARNING ABILITY APPEARS HIGH (PAVLOVIAN
TESTING)
WING BEATS PER SECOND 420 (WORKER)
EUROBEE 500 (WORKER)
FLIGHT SPEED 12 MPH (WORKER) (DEADWIND)
EUROBEE 14 MPH (WORKER) (DEADWIND)
EXTENDED
FLIGHT RANGE 100 MILES
EUROBEE 29 MILES
```

"Ask for a check," Wood said, staring at the screen. McAllister pecked at the keyboard. The computer repeated:

```
EXTENDED FLIGHT RANGE 100 MILES
EUROBEE 29 MILES
VIBRATION TOLERANCE LOW
FECUNDITY RATE HIGH
REPRODUCTIVE RATE HIGH
VENOM TOXICITY LEVEL HIGH
ABSCONDING POTENTIAL HIGH
ELITISM CHARACTERISTIC HIGH
ROBBING PROPENSITY HIGH
HURTROPISM HIGH
EUSOCIOLITY HIGH
SWARMING TENDENCY HIGH
POPULATION GROWTH POTENTIAL HIGH
END END END
```

The screen went blank. "That wraps up the size question," Wood said. "It's not venom or aggressiveness that's involved so much as the ability to travel. His survival mechanism is spread—farther and faster than even the African bees in Brazil can travel."

"How did you establish the flight range?" Gerston asked McAllister.

"Suspended a bee on a string and had it fly against a jet of air. What endurance! You understand he wouldn't fly a hundred miles at a clip. He'd have to stop and rest. But he can cover a lot of ground when he's swarming."

150

Wood said, "That sounds like the African bee, all right."

"And being larger, he has more storage space to carry food," McAllister added. "Some swarms might fly great distances. Or they could get a lift once the urge to move hits them—on a truck, a boat, a railroad car, even a plane. I imagine they can travel at night, at least on a moonlit night. They'd cover the country in no time at all. They'd be spread thin at first, but would start Africanizing the bees in the vicinity, colony by colony."

Maria said, "That squares exactly with the bee-incident pattern."

"It's like a migrating tribe," Wood said. "The main body moves slowly, but it's constantly sending out small groups in advance. I suppose the 'elitism' mentioned in the ethogram means that the big Africans, with their pronounced tendency to spread out, would be the 'opinion makers' in the hives—the rulers. They'd lead and the others would follow. It's a group effect."

"That's true of normal bees," McAllister said. "The others follow without question, because a hive is eusocial."

"I give up," Gerston said. "What is 'eusocial'?"

"A high degree of cooperation within the colony. Those mutants have it even more than ordinary bees."

"They're like scientists, then," Gerston said, laughing sarcastically.

"Forgive me, but I'm a foreigner. What is 'hurtropism'?" Maria asked. "Something to do with pain?"

Wood said, "Fess up, McAllister. You coined it."

"Not exactly. It has to do with fire. The Africans are attracted by fire. But I meant more than that. They are drawn by bright, flickering lights."

A thought flashed in and out of Wood's mind before he could grasp it.

"Shall I sum up?" McAllister went on before they broke.

151

"This insect is a very tough customer, determined to spread out and able to cooperate effectively with others of his kind. That's an enormous advantage." He stared at the screen. "I'm beginning to wonder if this is a battle science can win."

"Of course we'll win," Wood said angrily.

The tense mood was broken by the arrival of a uniformed soldier carrying a tray with small glasses. "Compliments of Dr. Hubbard, sir," he said to Wood. "I'm supposed to tell you it's bread."

Wood relaxed and smiled. "Beebread. It's the new high-protein compound developed by NASA, which our bees will eat instead of pollen."

Gerston took a sip of the white fluid and wrinkled his long face. "I'm glad I'm not a bee—or an astronaut."

At the door Wood whirled suddenly. "Where do you find concentrations of bright, flickering lights? I'll tell you where—the cities. That's something we must not forget."

15

PRESSURE

During his first hectic days at Detrick John Wood came to understand the other scientists better than people he had known his whole life. It was not merely a matter of working with them fourteen hours a day; he also had a chance to see them under the condition in which the basic outline of a human personality becomes as clear as the lines on a rubbing—stress.

Shelly Hubbard, for instance. Wood had served under Hubbard at the Academy for five years, yet only now did he see the beetle in full perspective. Wood could only marvel that Hubbard had let himself be desk-bound for so long. The zoologist was like a genie released from a bottle. He was everywhere. Time after time, when problems arose that seemed insurmountable, Hubbard's energy, inventiveness and brillance found the way. Under stress Hubbard prospered, or seemed to.

He performed still another service too—one Wood was to remember—that of morale-building. It was Hubbard who kept encouraging them when their spirits sank. Hubbard had a gimmick. At the morning sessions he would sometimes appear wearing his Eisenhower jacket from World War II. Making the squishing noise with his hands, his antennalike projections of hair standing out from his dome of a head, Hubbard would say to them, "Hang in. We'll do this job, you'll see. Don't forget, our enemy is an insect. He may be a fearsome insect, but he is still an insect. In no sense is he a match for man."

Wood revered Sheldon Hubbard, but he was aware that the beetle's gruff decisiveness and demanding ego could be abrasive to some. A sensitive individual such as George Fine, for instance.

Fine, who seemed to possess limited physical strength, must have paid a high price for driving himself so hard. He was a shy, solitary man who spoke seldom and kept his feelings to himself. Wood liked Fine but wrote in his mental notebook a word of warning. Fine, the nit-picker, would have to be prodded. And he would have to be watched. His secretiveness could lead him to keep vital details to himself, details others should know.

The only scientist about whom Wood had serious worries was Walter Krim. Not about his abilities; again and again Krim's intelligence illuminated critical areas. But something was bothering Krim, something that went beyond the young geneticist's obvious (and, to Wood, somewhat silly) sensitivity to his height, something that had always been there but that was being stirred up at Detrick by the pressure all of them were under now. Occasionally Wood caught a strange, remote gleam in Krim's eyes. Behind the brittle outer rim of his intelligence, Wood was sure, Krim festered.

As for John Wood, that he was a natural leader became clearer every day. Under pressure he performed well. But he had to use self-control to conceal from the scientists how apprehensive he really felt. He had a boundless faith in science's ability to function when it understood the problems. Was this one, he secretly wondered, beyond their capacity to comprehend?

When Wood first arrived at Detrick, he had toured the fort by car, examining other installations there for possible use by B Group. He had noticed a large building in front of which was a sign reading "Be Alert for Hazards Everywhere" and another over the doorway announcing that this was the U.S. Army Strategic Communications Command, East Coast Telecommunications Center. Then Wood recalled that Slater had mentioned such a facility. On impulse, he went inside.

A duty officer explained that the upper floors housed a computerized army communications headquarters. On one part of the main floor was a radio setup called MARS.

"What's MARS?" Wood wanted to know.

"Military Affiliate Radio System," the officer returned. "It serves as a semipublic radio network between military bases in the U.S. Also, servicemen abroad can speak to their families at home on MARS radio. In conditions of national emergency, MARS can operate as a disaster network."

Interested, Wood asked, "How does that work?"

"MARS has a club of ham radio operators, some 5,000 of them. They can use the MARS frequencies, and we can relay messages from here." He pointed to a bank of equipment bearing the letters WAR. "That's us—Whiskey Alpha Romeo."

Probing further, Wood learned that the hams could provide a unique, instant, widespread reporting service outside normal communications channels. And many ham operators were located in isolated places. It now occurred to John Wood that the hams could be asked to flash messages concerning bee incidents anywhere in the United States, and a 24-hour Bee Watch went into service at Detrick on the MARS frequencies.

This was one reason why B Group was far better informed about the situation than the news media and the general public. It also helped explain why B Group felt under increasing pressure. For the map in the command room, where incidents were recorded, was starting to fill up.

Henry David felt under pressure, too, and from a quarter he liked least, the government. It was largely because of his hatred of government that he had fled the world, and here was the government at his very door.

A state agricultural worker was supposed to visit him once a year to check his colonies for diseases; in actual fact the inspectors came far less frequently. But since the attack on Maryville, only weeks before, the inspectors had come frequently to look for the bees, and they had taken several colonies away with them. Like many beekeepers, David gave the bees sulfathiozole and Terramycin to protect them against foulbrood. He was told to start now instead of waiting until after the honey flow as usual. But he had no intention of complying. The honey would be rendered unfit to eat. What the processors did with honey was bad enough already. Boiling it, they ruined the natural flavor.

Now, at dusk, he heard a sound, and looking out his trailer window, he saw a flashing red light coming down the dirt road. The police, he thought, but outside he was amazed to find a small truck with "U.S. Army" stenciled on the side. There were two soldiers and both wore side arms.

"Mr. David?" one soldier said politely. He carried his cap in his hand.

"I am Henry David."

"I'm sorry to bother you, sir. I have a purchase order here for some bees."

Henry David was confused. "Purchase order?"

"Yes, sir." The soldier looked at the paper he held in his hand, squinting in the dim light. "It says here 'dumb bees.' "

"Dumb bees," David repeated. He recalled having told someone about them—oh, yes, the scientist fellow at Maryville. "The bees that like pollen but gather no honey?"

"I suppose so, sir. Which bees are they?"

"In back of the trailer." Something in the soldier's quick expression made David sorry he had given away their location. "They're my pets. I don't want to sell them."

"I was told you would want to sell them," the soldier said. He clearly meant *must* sell them.

"I don't want to," David said stubbornly.

"I don't think you understand, sir." Now Henry David grasped the significance of the firearm. "My instructions are to bring back the bees." He handed Henry David a green U.S. Treasury check in the amount of five hundred dollars.

Not another word was exchanged. The soldiers carried screens. They screened the hives and carried them to the truck, which disappeared down the road. Henry David felt alone and troubled. He missed his little pals already. Whatever was to become of them, he was sure they would not like it. He stared at the long, even rows of quiet beehives in front of the trailer. Suddenly his beeyard reminded him of a cemetery.

Krim's job was to try to introduce genetic defects, or negative survival characteristics, into the Africans. There were two general ways to proceed, each unsatisfactory. The first was to try to produce, through X-rays, ultraviolet light, or chemicals, mutant bees that might then be crossbred with the Africans. Here the trouble was that Krim had no way of knowing what kind of mutation he would get, or whether it would be passed along. The second way was to find a mutant strain of bees and cross their genetic material with the Africans'. Though Krim could not be sure that the defective strain would be strong enough to produce mutant Africans, this was the method he decided to use.

Impatiently Krim waited for the shipment of droopy-winged bees that had been sent air express from the experimental bee lab at Davis, California. Arrival day came and went, with no bees. Krim got on the phone. The bees had been sent. Two days later they were found in a freight room at Dulles Airport. Krim was right to explode. The bees delivered to Detrick were dead.

It was Gerston who had thought of the "dumb" bees during the morning meeting.

"Why 'dumb'?" Krim wanted to know.

"That's what the old beekeeper called them. He's profoundly right too. These bees gather pollen but no honey, and therefore must be dumb in the deepest sense of the word. They couldn't survive a week without outside help. Creatures that set up the conditions for their own destruction can only be described as stupid."

David's bees were requisitioned and arrived at once. In the experimental hive McAllister performed preliminary tests on these new bees on a crash basis. They were a strange combination—gentle with humans, hostile to other bees, and profoundly stupid.

Now Krim could get started. Genetic surgery was in its infancy; scientists only barely understood how it worked. There were almost no technological guidelines to follow. The job would be enormously complex, and Krim was exhausted already.

"What's the time factor?" Gerston asked with a concerned look.

Krim said in his garbled voice, "If the queens mate with the Africans and make it into African hives, they could be responsible for two or three generations of defective bees by the end of the summer. I'd say the negative survival characteristic ought to show up in the next few months, if it appears at all."

The same urgency was experienced by George Fine.

Edgewood Arsenal had been sticky but finally understood the situation and issued Fine the proper clearance. ZP-10960A, it revealed, had the chemical name of *neodiisophrophyl phosphorofluoridate*. Fine understood what that meant.

This chemical belonged to a class of substances that affected the body by interfering with the function of acetylcholinesterase (AChE). AChE, as he had pointed out to Wood, breaks down the acetylcholine released at nerve endings, which results in an impulse. If these impulses are not terminated, the impulses continue to be sent, and the body and brain go out of control. Heart rhythm, for instance, is regulated by AChE, and if AChE production is lowered or stopped, the heart begins to beat irregularly, causing death.

Before World War II only "reversible" anticholinesterase (anti-ChE) agents were known. "Reversible" meant that the conditions caused by the chemical could be reversed by the body unless it had been received in a large amount. The effect then was temporary. Reversible anti-ChE agents were found in poisons used by African tribes. At the beginning of World War II, I. G. Farben in Germany developed a new class of highly toxic chemicals, the organophosphates, first as pesticides, such as parathion, then as a chemical-warfare agent, namely, the famous nerve gas tabun. The extreme toxicity of this gas and its relatives, sarin and sonan, was due to their "irreversible" action on AChE, resulting in death.

Neodiisophrophyl phosphorofluoridate represented an interesting and important chemical breakthrough. Although the effects and chemical structure made it seem to belong to the highly toxic irreversible group of compounds, it was in fact a reversible agent if you knew the secret. Acute anti-ChE intoxication could be countered with a drug called atropine when used in sufficient dosages. Atropine did not work well against neodiisophrophyl phosphorofluoride, rendering the standard defense against nerve gases powerless. What did work, and effectively, was a substance developed at Edgewood called protoatropine.

Production of the new substance had been put on the shelf, partly because American warheads were already filled with effective chemical-warfare agents and partly because more peaceful relations with China and the Soviet Union made a development program for a new weapon seem increasingly

159

unnecessary. Nonetheless, Fine was sworn to the greatest secrecy. Only he among B Group knew precisely the nature of the chemicals he was dealing with. If anything happened to Fine, his successor would have to deal again with Edgewood.

Fine by now had ruled out the development of an antitoxin to the bee venom. It might take years. What he wanted was an antidote that could be placed in an ampule for autoinjection and widely distributed. But before anything was said, protoatropine had to be tested. It might not work, because neodiisophrophyl phosphorofluoridate was in a new combination with bee venom.

Fine made his first tests with white rabbits. He gave the rabbits an injection of venom, and followed it up at varying intervals with protoatropine. The first rabbit died before Fine could give it the antidote. He lowered the venom dosage and gave it to another rabbit. This one lived long enough to receive the antidote, but only just.

In this way he gradually established the antidote's capacity to stop venom action in rabbits. The first tests were satisfactory. He then proceeded to a larger animal, a dog. Next would come rhesus monkeys, which left one step to go—testing the antidote on a human being. He wondered who; inevitably, there would be some risk.

"CQ, Fort Detrick, Maryland . . . CQ, Fort Detrick, Maryland . . . CQ, Fort Detrick, Maryland. This is Whiskey, Eight, Alpha, Bravo, Charlie. CQ, Fort Detrick, Maryland . . . CQ, Fort Detrick, Maryland."

The Detrick operator, a sergeant, had been spinning the dial across the band to pick up transmissions emanating from anywhere in the country. When he heard Whiskey, Eight, Alpha, Bravo, Charlie calling he locked in on the frequency.

"Hello W8ABC. This is Whiskey, Three, Whiskey, Alpha, Romeo, Fort Detrick, Maryland," the operator said in a bored voice.

"W3WAR, this is W8ABC. I'm Harry Brandon on Deer Island. I'm in trouble, W3WAR, bad trouble."

The sergeant looked at the duty officer, who put down a paperback novel and stared across the room.

"What's the trouble, W8ABC? Where exactly is Deer Island?"

The duty officer signaled to a soldier at a switchboard. It was possible to trace the location of a sending station. The officer had started this procedure just in case.

"You've never heard of it. It's a small island in Lake Superior, just offshore. I'm about forty miles from Duluth, to the northeast."

"Okay, W8ABC. We've found you. What's the trouble?"

"There's a tremendous swarm of bees outside. They seem to want to get in. I can hardly believe it."

The sergeant glanced at the officer, who said, "Ask if he's called for help." The sergeant did.

"This is my call for help. There's no phone."

"Where are you on the island, W8ABC?"

"Southern tip. You can't miss it. Only house. Send a helicopter. Send something." Brandon was frightened.

The officer began looking up the nearest military base that had a helicopter.

"In motion, W8ABC. Are you alone?"

"Yes. I came over to do some fishing. Oh God."

"What is it, W8ABC?"

"They're beating on the windows. Sounds like a hailstorm."

"Any place to hide, W8ABC? Have you a cellar?"

"No cellar. This is just a summer shack." There was a sound like glass breaking. Brandon said, "Oh God, here they come." He began to scream.

The duty officer and the sergeant looked at each other and for a few seconds froze. The sergeant turned back to the microphone.

"Come in W8ABC. Come in, W8ABC. Come in Whiskey, Eight, Alpha, Bravo, Charlie," the sergeant repeated endlessly. *"Can you hear me? Can you hear me?"*

16

THE "COCKTAIL"

The aim had been to insulate the scientists from the terror sweeping the country, just as the country tried to protect itself from the dangerous bees. In vain were both efforts. Fear floated into the inner compound at Detrick as if borne on wings.

McAllister's sister called the entomologist from a small town north of Chicago. She neither knew nor cared what experiment her brother was conducting in Maryland. It mattered only that, as a bee man, he could tell her what to do.

Rose and her family lived across the street from tennis courts. Between sobs she related what she had witnessed from her window. She had not even had time to shout warning.

A bulldozer had been clearing ground for new courts when the bees came, silently, as if from nowhere, massing above the courts unseen until a player lobbed and, raising his head, saw the tennis ball enter the black patch. He screamed. The bees descended with the ball.

Some players made it to the gates, but most got only to the fence. One man shinnied up and over in terrible haste as if breaking from prison; another, halfway up, stiffened as though the fence had electrocuted him and dropped to the hard surface below. Others flailed their rackets in a desperate game with the lunging bees.

Six died.

McAllister's counsel to his sister consisted of one word: "Move."

But the letter Gerston received affected the Detrick scientists still more. It had been forwarded unopened in a larger envleope by Gerston's wife, who enclosed a photograph of their daughter. Gerston yelped delightedly, passing the picture around the control room, but when he looked at the letter his long face puckered.

"God," he gasped, and read the letter aloud. It was from a male cousin who taught college in New Mexico.

. . . never been through anything so horrible. A dozen people, half of them children, swam in a pool. I'd been playing around with my kid's face mask and breathing tube, thank God! The only warning was this whir—like the rustling of distant leaves. I guess those goddamn bees wanted water, because they dipped to the pool. The kids naturally panicked, and splashed water at them. It was the wrong thing to do.

There were people around the pool, and seeing what was happening, they ran away. Two adults in the pool got out and tried to run, but didn't get far. The rest of us stayed where we were.

Even letting the top of your head show above water was risky. I could stay down because of the tube, but the others had to come up for air. I watched some of it, though. Lucky I had the mask—a couple of bees banged against the glass.

First we all went into shallow water—except one kid, trying to swim, didn't make it. She wore water wings, and for the next two hours her corpse floated around the pool like some awful buoy, still getting stung. The rest of us squatted in the water, sticking our heads out like seals and taking huge gasps of air, and then ducking under again. I hate to say this, but the bees seemed to catch on. When a face emerged they tried to sting it. I can't communicate the horror of people trying to breathe before the bees got them—these helpless faces darting out and the bees diving at them. One man had this enormous red swelling on his cheek and one eye was closed. Actually, he survived—one of three. The police didn't dare use gas on the bees because of us, so there was no defense whatever. Finally the bees flew away.

Bob, you're an entomologist. Do something before it's too late for all of us.

The scientists drew long breaths. Wood said, "Did you see *The New York Times?*" He pointed to the editorial.

THE AFRICAN CALAMITY

The President in his statement of three weeks ago reassured the nation on the menace of the African honeybee. He called it "small," instructed the nation not to panic, and said that scientific experts would soon have the situation under control.

Clearly, the secrecy cannot be maintained much longer. The nation has a right to know what measures are being undertaken for its defense.

Clearly, too, the menace posed by these insect invaders is mounting. Reports from over the country tell of attacks by these savage creatures and growing apprehension on the part of the public.

It seems to us entirely conceivable that the dangerous bee— whose venom can be fatal—could so disrupt agriculture in the United States that food shortages and even starvation could result. Cities such as New York are entirely dependent on the outside for food and are thus especially vulnerable.

Urban areas should be stockpiling food now. But they are not. There is a pervasive optimism about science's capacity to deal with this intruder, but we wonder how much this confidence is justified.

Can this bee really be stopped? Could it conceivably render this continent uninhabitable for human beings? To such momentous questions the nation must have answers—and soon.

"Let's talk about the cocktail," Wood said tersely.

The "cocktail" fell under a category called "alternatives to pesticides."

As Wood pointed out, the first defensive weapon used by man against his insect enemies was his own hand. Until technology brought the insecticide into being, nothing could compete with the human hand in terms of plain effectiveness.

The most famous—or infamous—of pesticides is DDT, an odorless, colorless, crystalline compound first synthesized in 1874 but not recognized as an insecticide until the early 1940s. Its first notable successes were against clothes moths and lice in Swiss refugee camps. It was used on a large scale against a lice-borne typhus epidemic in Italy during World War II, with staggering effectiveness. By the mid-1960s American manufacturers were producing 180 million pounds of DDT a year—by far the record for a pesticide before or since.

DDT was thought to be the "final solution" to the problem of harmful insects. But, as Wood knew, even before Rachel Carson's *Silent Spring* called international attention to the dangers of DDT to man and the environment, thoughtful biologists had warned that insects would soon develop an immunity to the substance. Further, they said, this immunity would be hereditary. And within a few years after DDT was used on a mass scale, mosquitoes, house flies and other insects began to be impervious to it. In the Tennessee Valley, flies became DDT-resistant in a matter of months. It was also learned that the DDT in the environment was increasingly hazardous to man.

There was another class of pesticides available, the organophosphates, which had the same chemical structure as nerve gases. They degraded more rapidly than DDT, but they were much more immediately toxic than DDT to man and animals.

All along scientists had been interested in pesticide alternatives, but spurred by ecologists such as Wood, the search accelerated.

One promising technique was sterilization. In 1916 the entomologist G. A. Runner reported the sterilization of cigarette beetles with X-rays. It was then learned that insects could be sterilized and still not lose the desire to mate. At the U.S. Department of Agriculture a technique was devised by which male screwworm flies were raised in captivity, exposed to cobalt-60 radiation, and dropped by airplane over the island of Curaçao and screwworm-infested areas in Florida. They mated with females, which produced infertile eggs. So successful was this program that it is still carried out in Texas, where, during the screwworm mating season, the USDA raises and releases 150 million sterilized males a week.

For a number of reasons—among them that not all sterilized male insects can compete with unsterilized males—new and highly original pesticide alternatives have been tried. Wood reviewed them.

One, Wood said, involved the manipulation of insect growth patterns. In 1920, investigating the transformation to gypsy moth from the caterpillar stage, Polish biologist Stephan Kopec tied a slender cord around the caterpillar's middle. The head section molted and pupated normally, but the tail section remained that of a caterpillar. There must be, Kopec deduced, a developmental substance whose passage from the anterior section had been blocked. His microsurgical experiments established the existence of such a substance, a hormone.

Another biologist, a Japanese, Soichi Fuka, found a second hormone, without which neither molting nor pupating occurred. He called it ecdysone, from the Greek *ekdysis,* meaning "escape." Still a third controlling hormone was discovered by the English physiologist V. B. Wigglesworth. It was called simply the juvenile hormone.

Injections of ecdysone brought insects through growth and development at a breakneck pace, resulting in premature death. When the juvenile hormone was administered, larvae either did not metamorphose or grew into intermediate forms incapable of reproduction.

But the hormones would have to be synthesized if they were to be employed on a large scale for insect control. In 1966 a simple chemical process was discovered to produce a synthetic

167

hormone that, when put into water at a ratio of one part to 100,000, completely prevented the emergence of adult mosquitoes.

Finally it was found that hormonal substances that distorted insect growth could be developed from trees and plants. In 1964 a young Czech entomologist, Karel Slama, working at Harvard, hit on the fact that larvae placed on paper toweling failed to mature, while those not exposed to the toweling did. The "paper factor" was traced to the balsam tree, used in all American paper manufacture. It was deduced that plants might use mimic insect hormones as their own means of encouraging or controlling insects. Further, the mimic ecdysones isolated from trees and plants proved to be specific. They acted upon some insects but not on others.*

In 1973, Wood noted, the Department of Agriculture, in experiments with line-rearing of bees, discovered that an ecdysone made from goldenrod would speed the development of bees. Administered in larger quantities than the bees would receive from nature, it produced giant larvae that failed to mature.

There were also the pheromones. Wood traced the history of this discovery.

It had been long known that insects attract each other for mating purposes by means of smell. In 1890 the French naturalist Jean-Henri Fabre proved that a species of moth could attract the opposite sex in the dark. Fabre, however, comparing the atmosphere to a huge sink, did not believe such an event could occur over any great distance as a result of odor particle. Instead, he assumed the moths communicated by radio waves, and in this he was mistaken. Subsequently it was learned that the male silkworm moth can detect the chemical attractant

---

* An article especially helpful to Wood was Dr. Morton Grosser's "The Control of Insects," *Zoecon Corporation 1970 Annual Report.*

secreted by the female from a distance of 6.8 miles, orienting itself to the female's location against the wind.

Not merely sex attraction, scientists found, but a number of insect activities were governed by chemical messengers, which were called pheromones, from the Greek *pherein* ("to carry") and *horman* ("to excite"). They were chemical hot lines carrying information vital to survival. They included, in the case of bees, alarm (sending the soldiers to battle), aggregation (or colony cohesion), trail marking, recognition (through hive odors), and the nuptial flight of queens. The queen bee alone secretes over thirty kinds of chemical messengers from glands in her head and thorax.

The cocktail, as Wood and his fellow scientists designed it, would carry three ingredients—an antipheromone substance, an insect growth regulator, and a disease that killed bees.

The U.S. Department of Agriculture's experimental research station at Beltsville, Maryland, was able to locate quickly a large apiary outside Baltimore where American foulbrood had broken out. AFB causes infected larvae to shrivel and die. Infected larvae from ten hives contained enough AFB spores to infect every beehive in the world.

The insect growth regulator (IGR) was manufactured by Zoecon, a California company that specialized in insecticide alternatives. To produce IGR on the scale necessary demanded a thousand-gallon capacity, which Zoecon had.

The antipheromone proved the hardest until Wood, in the discussion, remembered that spiders exposed to a certain substance lost the ability to build webs. The chemical was LSD.

McAllister thought that minute quantities of LSD introduced into the experimental hives might cause the bees to run about aimlessly, forgetting to feed the queen or build comb for the young. Experiments soon proved him correct. Wood believed the LSD would have to be microencapsulated in order to give

169

the bees that swallowed it time enough to get back to the hive, but experiments subsequently showed that the bees would return to the hive before the drug took effect.

LSD, AFB spores and IGR would be put into honey. The honey went into small plastic receptacles that would break open but not shatter on impact. The cocktails—to be manufactured by Du Pont in Delaware, which could turn them out in three weeks—would be dropped by the hundreds of thousands over African enclaves. The bees would eat the honey, fly back to the hives, and add the regurgitated honey to their stores. In the hive, AFB would attack the larvae, the hormones would also attack the larvae, and the LSD would disrupt hive activity. A bee colony must have homeostasis—that is, it must maintain a steady state of self-regulation through internal feedback. LSD would change homeostasis to anarchy.

As Wood remarked to the group when the planning session was over, it seemed easy—almost too easy.

17

A CASUALTY AT DETRICK

Despite the mounting pressure, each scientist performed the tasks assigned to him and tried to help the others as well. Much of this work would be wasted—which they knew and accepted. As Hubbard liked to say, in scientific research you paid your nickel and took your chances.

Sheldon Hubbard had good reason to be satisfied, for his bee factory was rolling. The queens in the laying area were performing like troopers. More than 16,000 had survived, and each day they filled 16,000 plastic platens with eggs. Attendants in sterilized laboratory gear—blue, white or brown, depending on which line they serviced—moved the trays on metal carts to the incubators where the eggs would hatch. As soon as the incubators were empty, they were cleaned and filled with freshly laid eggs, so the process of reproduction and development continued without pause.

On the surface, Hubbard himself seemed unchanged, making the squishing noise with his hands, bobbing his beetle head with its antennalike projections of hair. Deep down, though, Hubbard was bone tired. He had gone without sufficient food or sleep for weeks as he prodded the construction along. He had not told anyone, but for the first time in his life he had begun to suffer from dizzy spells. He was not young anymore, he told himself; as soon as the first queens emerged from the blue line he would slow up. But in the meantime there was so much to do. . . .

The Grid Area at Fort Detrick looks from the air like a giant target, with large concentric circles around the center. Over this target a HUEY helicopter hovered, dropping light plastic boxes from various heights.

Each of these boxes, fluttering to the ground, contained live American bees. McAllister, in a bee veil, checked the condition of the insects as dropped from different heights. Some of the boxes contained the alarm pheromone—isopentyl acetate—in glass vials. These vials shattered on impact, and the bees rose from the boxes in an ugly mood, so ugly that McAllister and his assistants had turned and run. McAllister hoped they would rout the Africans in the same way.

Walter Krim, the young geneticist, found himself uncontrollably tense, even snappish. The experiment he was conducting was getting to him. The others, at least, would be able to tell within a reasonable time whether their work had succeeded, but Krim might not know for months. He might never know.

The line-reared queens were to be made "stupid" and then released. They had to mate successfully with African drones, breed, and their progeny mate and breed too, before self-destructively stupid bees would exist in numbers large enough to make a difference. Perhaps two generations would be required, perhaps three. It might not happen until the end of the summer, or even later. It might not happen at all. Genes were a tricky business.

Normally, Krim would have tested the procedure on generations of bees under laboratory conditions, but there was no time for that. He would have liked to run a computerized study on

172

probability outcomes, but in view of the pressure, decided to wait for that. Either it worked or it didn't, Krim told himself fatalistically.

There was, however, certain knowledge that he had to have, and Mac McAllister provided it. He made a hasty visit to Henry David to ask questions and conducted tests in the 8-ball, combining the information into an ethogram. Though the dumb strain reappeared generation after generation, it had not spread over Henry David's hives; the reason, it seemed, lay not in their lack of fecundity but in the odd hours the queer bees chose for mating flights. Finally, as McAllister showed, the drones of this tribe were strong and far-ranging.

These qualifications were vital. A recessive gene would have failed to do the job, and so would low fertility. That the dumb bees picked funny times to mate didn't matter, Krim thought; it was a quirk of a minor sort that would be drowned in the African gene pool.

About this gene Walter Krim made one highly sophisticated assumption on which the experiment might stand or fall. He chose to interpret the bees' peculiar habit of gathering pollen but no honey as a symptom, not a trait on its own. The genetic trait that lay behind this habit Krim saw as a sort of urge to racial suicide, and this, rather than any one manifestation of the genetic defect, was what Krim wanted to transmit to the Africans.

The technique known variously as "genetic surgery," "genetic transfers," "genetic manipulation," "genetic engineering," and the "genetic hook" had been talked about since the mid-1940s. Scientists at Rockefeller Institute (now Rockefeller University) in New York City succeeded in extracting genetic material from one kind of cell and putting it into another, giving that cell new hereditary properties. But the technique was crude; the injected material consisted of a mixture of many genes of various types. By the 1960s Rockefeller scientists had learned to break up the genetic material of a bacterial cell into individual genes, isolating specific ones that determined particular cell characteristics.

It was clear by then that there was a genetic language used by all forms of life on the planet, with minor variations. Simple genetic messages could be chemically synthesized, and genetic surgery was a reality applied to microorganisms. Genes from one strain of bacteria could be inserted into another. The host would then have received a new set of instructions, or genetic messages, whose commands, being now part of its physical self, had to be followed. Thus the nature of microorganisms could be changed.

Eventually, it was hoped, genetic surgery could be used to correct such human defects as mental retardation, diabetes, or sterility by introducing missing genes whose absence accounted for the trouble. The best approach seemed to be viruses. A virus consists of an outer shell and an inner core of the genetic code material, DNA. What a virus does is to enter a cell and force that cell to reproduce the virus.

The genetic transfer had already been accomplished in experiments with fruit flies at Iowa State. The trouble lay in imprecision. It was, so far, impossible to make the hook selective—that is, to make the virus pick up just the package of chromosomes wanted, and only those.

Now Krim was pushing the technique one step farther. His reasoning would be studied for years to come by intelligent scientists, but it could be boiled down to this: Since the virus was in essence pure DNA, what was the difference between a virus and DNA? Perhaps none. The dumb bees from Maryville may have had a virus once that entered their cellular system and located there permanently, lowering their intelligence. This virus was no longer transmissible by ordinary means, but it still existed as part of the bees' genetic code. Therefore, a virus would not be needed to spread "dumbness." The quality could be transmitted by using the genetic material of the dumb bees itself. The transfer would be direct, not by means of a viral intermediary.

This was the route Krim decided to take. Henry David's dumb bees ended their lives in a crusher and emerged as paste. This tissue was carefully reduced by a series of millicron filters and washings in a weak benzene. The clear fluid was filtered again, and what remained was a dab of white material that looked something like plastic. This was pure DNA. It was cultured by a standard system and grew. It was then brought to the National Institutes of Health near Washington, which cultured it in quantity. It would then be added to the royal jelly fed to the queen larvae in the bee factory. If it took, the viral-DNA residue would invade the cells of the larval queens, and they in turn would produce dumb bees. *If* it took . . .

Maria Amaral had been lent to Krim to help in the experiment. The two worked side by side in the lab, mostly in silence. Occasionally, when Krim wasn't looking, Maria watched him—apprehensively. Sometimes, too, Krim's uncertain glance stole toward her, but his expression was different. Behind the closed shutters of his mind Walter Krim was having fantasies—fantasies too urgent to ignore. In one he implanted his own genetic material in Maria Amaral. In another he was injected with bad seed.

George Fine, testing the antidote, had completed the series on dogs. Anesthetized with sodium pentobarbitol, they were injected with venom and then the antidote. Electrodes were attached from the dog to a physiograph that recorded EKG, heart rate, blood pressure, central venous pressure, respiration and electroencephalographs, while Fine observed impatiently. If one of these vital functions began to fail, Fine injected more proto-atropine. It did not always work. More than twenty purebred beagles had died in the experiments.

Fine was trying to determine what constituted a lethal dosage of venom in order to know how much antidote had to be used in the ampule or subsequent autoinjector. "LD 100" meant that all the animals died; "LD 50" that half of them did. Thus the dogs received the venom in various quantities, and Fine checked their functions with his instruments in terms of both lethality and time.

At last Fine determined how much antidote a dog required. The next series would use rhesus monkeys, whose physiology closely resembled that of a human. Then came the critical test, with a human volunteer. In the BW days at Detrick the army had what it called Project White Coat, in which soldiers, often Seventh Day Adventists, who are opposed to bloodshed, volunteered, after a fashion, to serve as guinea pigs. There would be no army volunteers now. Perhaps, Fine thought, something could be worked out with a convict in exchange for a parole. He no longer expected the experiment to be dangerous, but there was always the chance that something could go wrong.

Using live drones, Gerston—with Wood helping him—tested the sterilization procedures. The experiment had already proved successful: test drones exposed to radiation on their first day of adulthood survived, but the sperm they carried was useless to a queen. Now it was merely a matter of determining how many drones could be sterilized in the large room previously used for biological warfare. The walls consisted of a foot of lead encased in three feet of concrete.

The bees, in plastic boxes, had been placed on glass tables at various levels around the room. His footsteps echoing through the chamber, Gerston positioned the dosimeters—packets of lithium fluoride that would register radiation and indicate any blind spots. The proper dosage, it had been determined, was 50,000 roentgens of gamma radiation from cobalt-60 sources.

There were six sources buried in the concrete floor, capped by heavy lead shields. The cobalt-60 itself was attached to each of these shields. The shields fitted exactly into lead wells. Metal cables reached from the shields to the ceiling.

The two men left the room, closing the thick door with the electronic controls. The control panel was under a large yellow and maroon sign saying *Danger—Radiation*. When Gerston pressed a switch, shields carrying their cargoes of cobalt rose to varying heights in the room. Fifteen minutes later Gerston turned off the switch, and the cobalt sources slowly settled back into the crypts in the floor.

Gerston and Wood went into the room. As though a cloud had settled in the barren chamber, the air was gray and sharp, with the crackly smell of ozone.

Gerston checked the drones. "Well, they survived. They'll have sperm, but their mates won't produce workers—only drones."

"And if we're lucky, that'll be the end of the African hives."

They stared at each other. The tall entomologist said, "John, you seem worried. It isn't like you."

Wood stopped smiling. "Maybe I am a little. You see right through me, Bob."

"Well, don't worry. We'll nail those bees. You know, I'm starting to hate them."

"It wasn't the Africans I was thinking of," Wood said. "It's our own people. We're working too hard. We're all tired. Somebody will make a mistake."

In the third-floor bedroom John and Maria used, the radio carried the news: "Peculiar stories nobody quite knows the meaning of. Attacks by bees in many parts of the country, though principally in the northeast, north-mid-central area and the northwest. People in these regions have been urged by the Secretary of Agriculture, M. R. Voight, to carry bee veils and gloves with them at all times. Bees are to be avoided if possible, he says, and any bees of exceptional size should be reported at once. Voight maintains there is no serious cause for alarm, but no one here in Washington can remember a time when the government has taken such a keen interest in an insect. Swarms of bees have been sighted in flight, one of which, near southern Oregon, was so large that it was mistaken for a flock of migrating birds. We don't know what it adds up to, but—"

"Turn that damn thing off, will you?" John said from the barrackslike room's sole chair near the single window.

Maria rolled across the bed and switched off the radio. "We are grumpy tonight," she laughed.

"We are not grumpy. We are edgy, that's all," John said.

"Then we must remove the edge. Come here," she commanded.

She wore a pair of his pajama pants and was naked to the waist. Her dark hair, piled up during the day, fell to the small of her back. The contrast between her daytime and nighttime selves was like her hair—up during the day, down at night— and always surprised him. Cerebral, collected, detached as a scientist, in the bedroom she slipped into another role as easily as she took off her shoes. "Lie down."

He did, and instantly relaxed as her hands moved over his skin. "That's delicious."

"Poor darling," she said thoughtfully. "The pressure on you is terrific."

"Well, I'm fortunate," he murmured. "I have an outlet. I have you."

"I do not like being described as an outlet," she said firmly.

"All right. Still, when I do tense up, I have you to calm me down. The others don't."

She rubbed harder, as though her fingers could feel the tension that surged through him again. "Easy," she said. "Everything will be all right."

"Will it? I feel I should be down there in the facility right now." He yawned. "But I'm glad I'm not."

"How is the edge?"

"Going."

"Don't lose all of it," Maria said. "I have need for you."

Maria's head was on his bare shoulder, her hair spread out on his chest almost as if it had been arranged there. Wood was burrowed deep into sleep. Then the phone rang. For a moment he forgot where he was. He looked blankly at the bare, cell-like chamber almost devoid of furniture, at the moonbeams flooding the shadeless window, at the dark head on his shoulder. His watch said just past midnight. Now he could hear the alarm trumpet.

The phone rang again, and this time Wood picked it up. Fine's voice was hoarse. "It's Hubbard," he gasped. "He . . . Come down to the hive."

Wood put on the bed light. Maria jerked up her head. "What?"

"Hubbard," he said. He dove into his coveralls and shoes and left the room.

In the experimental hive, workmen in protective clothing were inside an air lock struggling to open the door to a hive containing giant Africans. The door wouldn't budge at first because the thick body of Sheldon Hubbard blocked it. The alarm trumpet howled.

As best he could, Fine told Wood what had happened.

George Fine had gone to bed, but preoccupied with the problem of antidote, he couldn't sleep. He had gone back to the lab

179

with the idea of continuing the venom tests on rhesus monkeys.

Through the glass partition separating the various sections of the facility he had noticed Hubbard pacing distractedly, as though thinking out a problem. Fine thought that it probably had to do with speeding up development on the bee-rearing lines, which Hubbard still wanted to accomplish.

The man looked exhausted. Fine had not been fond of Shelly since their argument, but he told himself that Hubbard had better slow down if he expected to make it through the long summer. He knew he could have said the same thing about himself.

Fine went back to his microscope. When he raised his head again he saw that Hubbard had donned a protective suit. In violation of the rule not to enter the hive without an observer, Hubbard went inside. He carried a plastic case with a dish of honey in it, with the obvious intent of capturing a few bees for experimental purposes. Fine was curious and began watching him through the glass wall separating the experimental apiary from the lab.

Fine saw what happened next in helpless horror. Inside the hive Hubbard stopped and shook his head as if he were dizzy. Then he stumbled on a flower pot, lurched, and went down, his visor catching on the corner of the wooden hive. For a heavy man, Hubbard got up fast, and Fine, on his feet, could see why. Hubbard had a rip in his headpiece.

Disturbed by the impact, the bees rose too, circling Hubbard's head and trying to plant their stings in the smooth plastic of the suit. Fine, moving hurriedly toward the experimental hive, saw Hubbard make a terrible mistake. Instead of heading directly for the lock, he tried to cover the hole in the visor with his hand, and backed off slowly. Fine, now in the experimental hive section, watched what happened next with disbelief. Shelly Hubbard was opening his visor! A bee had evidently slipped inside the hood and Hubbard was trying to get it out.

It was at this exact moment that George Fine hesitated. There was an emergency button that sounded a trumpet throughout the factory area, and he pressed it. Another button would have released cyanide inside the hive, but Hubbard had his window open. Also, Fine was not wearing a protective suit. The only thing he might have done was to enter the lock and open the door for Shelly Hubbard, which would have been extremely dangerous for George Fine. Perhaps, in that instant available, Fine's mind returned to the row with Hubbard; in any case, a second later it was too late.

Hubbard panicked. Fine saw his mouth fly open as though in a huge grin. He was screaming a single word—"Help!" Hubbard now wrenched the handle to the door of the lock so hard that it broke off in his hand. He held it, looked at it, and then the bees attacked in mass.

Hubbard tried to protect his face with his gloved hands, then pressed his face against the door. Slowly, his face slid down the glass until he was on his knees, his eyes puffed but open. That was where he was when Wood arrived.

Workmen in protective suits forced the door and dragged Hubbard into the lock. The bees that followed them were killed with wire swatters. Maria came, examined Hubbard, and pronounced him dead.

Fine was close to tears. "I should have gone in, should have gone in."

Wood felt numb. "There was nothing you could have done," he said tonelessly.

Sheldon Hubbard's obituaries, filled with praise for his scientific accomplishments, failed to mention his current project, which was absurd. The need for secrecy had already ended.

On the way back from Shelly Hubbard's funeral, four days later, Wood suddenly began to sob behind the wheel of the car.

Maria put her hand on the back of his head and held it there. Wood kept his wet eyes on the road.

Approaching Detrick, they could see that something had happened. Traffic was backed up and horns screamed. A policeman got them through the crowd.

In the old days at Fort Detrick, vigils against BW had been carried on by the Quakers. Now there were pickets again. Some carried signs reading *Save the Bees,* others *Kill the Bees.* The two groups had lined up outside the Detrick gate. They were fighting.

18

THE ENEMY GROWS

A principal objective of the scientists trying to deal with the African invaders was to avoid the indiscriminate slaughter of bees. Such an event might bring on an agricultural crisis at least as serious as the one posed by the Africans.

The scientists at the bee facility reasoned that if the public remained unaware of the large scientific effort being mounted at Detrick it might continue to regard the African bees as a localized menace, and by the time the peril was public knowledge, effective control techniques would already be in operation, allowing the President to announce that a solution had been found. It was in their assumption that the bee crisis could be dealt with on a rational level that the scientists made their major mistake.

The man responsible for blowing B Group's cover was F. W. McAllister.

Understandably, the people of Frederick, Maryland, were curious about what went on behind the new fence circling Detrick's inner compound. Workmen who had been employed there could give no cogent explanation about what had been constructed, except that it had to do, of all things, with *bees*. Getting the facts on the facility at Detrick was a story assigned to the top reporter of the local paper, the *Frederick Post*.

Fort Detrick's own public-affairs bulletin had routinely reported the arrival of eminent scientists at the fort, with their names and academic affiliations. The reporter picked a name at random. Checking by phone with Kansas University, the reporter learned that F. W. McAllister was an entomologist, hymenopterist and apiologist. He was on an extended leave of absence from the university.

The reporter called McAllister directly. He said merely that Frederick was honored to have an outstanding entomologist in its midst, and that the *Post* would like a profile on McAllister covering his background and accomplishments. Would he consent to be interviewed? Foolishly, McAllister agreed.

McAllister must have had an intimation about what would happen, for he said nothing about the interview to Wood. He met the reporter at the officers' mess, and over lunch responded enough to the reporter's flattery to give him an inkling of what went on in the secured building. In a way an inkling was worse than the full truth. The reporter was also a stringer for the Associated Press. The next day—the morning after Shelly Hubbard's death—a sensationalized account of B Group made front pages throughout the country.

The president of the National Academy of Sciences conferred by phone with the President of the United States, and a hastily organized press conference was called for 2 P.M. in the Fort Detrick theater, after which the reporters were invited to tour the facilities.

Willard Lightower read a brief statement for the TV cameras and turned the meeting over to Wood, who, though profoundly disturbed about Hubbard's death, was determined not to show it.

Q. Do you maintain that the African bees can be stopped?

A. I do, yes. We have prepared some very effective countermeasures. One of these, a control mechanism we call the "bee cocktail," will shortly be dropped in large numbers by airplane

184

over the infected areas. We ought to know soon how effective it is. Then we have other biological defense mechanisms.

Q. Do you feel the bees will reach our major cities?

A. I think they will be exterminated long before that.

Q. Is it true that a member of your group has just been killed by the African bees?

A. Yes, I'm terribly sorry to say.

Q. What is your attitude toward American bees? Do you believe our bees are loyal?

A. That's one way to put it. We are doing everything in our power to preserve the safety of domestic bees in apiaries in the infected areas. We think this can be done. So far, most of the country is free of the African bees, so there is no major problem. When Africans do invade American hives, we're depending on beekeepers to kill them off. On the whole, I'm convinced that American bees can be saved.

Q. How many domestic beehives are there in the United States?

A. Something over four million, I believe.

Q. How many bees would that represent?

A. Oh, about two hundred billion, I guess.

Q. There are wild bees too?

A. Yes. In large numbers.

Q. So if they all sided with the Africans, we'd have quite a problem, wouldn't we?

A. Nothing remotely like that will happen, I promise you.

Q. Is it conceivable that we're in for some nasty surprises?

A. We've gone over the situation pretty carefully. I think we'll take care of the Africans according to plan.

Q. You mentioned "biological defense mechanisms." Does that rule out pesticides?

A. We have no plans to use insecticides at present. We think the situation can be stabilized without further upsetting the ecological balance by mass use of insecticides.

185

Q. Have you been working up defense measures with the Pentagon?

A. I'm not prepared to go into that as yet.

The response was almost immediate. Predictably, that same evening, following the TV news, the Save-the-Bees Coalition was born, founded by Perry Goodall, the New York public-relations man.

He called some friends. "Did you hear what the military is up to now? Boy, talk about your overreaction. Next thing, the Pentagon will be asking for a bigger budget. Won't you join with me to save the bees?"

Goodall had made contributions to certain politicians, who agreed to be listed on a letterhead. He designed a button and persuaded a leading author to write an article saying that the bee scare was the work of the CIA. He began raising money for a full-page ad in the *Times*.

The Kill-the-Bees Society was organized by Mrs. Adele Terrace, of Oyster Bay, Long Island, who had been stung by a bee and had not gotten over the shock.

Perhaps John Wood failed to be sufficiently precise, because Mrs. Terrace's impression was that the scientists were showing softness toward the bees. She did not want bees saved, she wanted them killed. After all, they stung.

Mrs. Terrace had once been a delegate to a national political convention, and she had friends over the country. Having decided to act, she did so with verve. She organized a group in Oyster Bay and had trunk lines installed in her living room. The calls went out.

These were the two groups Wood saw picketing and fighting before Fort Detrick the day of Hubbard's funeral. The national media saw them at once as news, and gave them far more space than they deserved at the time. Their leaders spoke and people listened. Fear won out over conservation; the message that got through loudest was "Kill the Bees."

Silently, furtively, with torches, they came from Maryville, a town that hated bees. While Henry David slept they set fire to his hives.

Henry David woke to the smell of burning wood and honey. The beeyard was set in a clearing, so there was no danger to his trailer or to the trees. But the apiary had been destroyed. From one end of the yard to the other the hives were burning like funeral pyres.

Henry David went back to bed and waited for dawn with his eyes open. His career was over—he could not start again. He had a little money and could move to Florida, but instinct told him that was not what he would do. He had always preferred bees to people.

When daylight came he rose, dressed and went outside, as he always did. Charred ruins in even rows awaited him. Usually at this hour the hives hummed with activity as the bees began the day's work, but this morning the clearing was quiet as a crypt.

Henry David felt a light touch on his hand and looked down in surprise. It was a bee. Suddenly there were two, then three, then four. He glanced up and saw that bunches of bees filled the trees—soundless, immobile bees. In some places the branches bent from the weight of hundreds of thousands of bunched bees. As he watched, bees detached themselves from the bunches and flew to him, settling on his arms, his shoulders, his head. They did not sting.

Little by little Henry David began to feel the weight, and then he understood. Peaceful, unafraid, he felt no urge to escape, even if he had been able. The bees were all over his face now, covering his eyes and nasal passages, gentle but implacable. He was becoming short of breath and his old shoulders stooped under the mounted bees. Almost caressingly, the bees brought the unprotesting Henry David to the ground.

Henry David felt honored, not betrayed. The bees reserved this rite for royalty. They were balling him, as they balled a queen.

Wood's prediction at the press conference—that no major surprises were in store—was bound up in the rationalistic way the scientists approached their problem. As far as they were concerned, they were dealing with an insect enemy; they had not foreseen that people might intervene in ways that made their task far harder.

Hundreds of beeyards were burned, mostly at night. But the attackers were ignorant about the daily routine of bees. During the nectar flow, bees do not sleep. Then a beehive is always active.

The very vibrations set up by the feet of the intruders would trigger the alarm system; the guards would alert the others. The first tendril of smoke would cause the bees to fill up on honey in anticipation of leaving their home. Then, as the fire spread, the bees streamed forth. Attacking the arsonists meant losing their lives for nothing; the hive was lost to the flames, and there was nothing left to defend. Instead, the bees escaped to the forest to save themselves.

But not the queen. Once she has started laying, a queen needs preparation, grooming, to fly. Perhaps she stayed in the hive and perished, wings burning. Perhaps she flew a few feet and dropped. Her absence was an important fact.

Many hiveless bees died, but many did not. During the nectar flow, colonies need workers; they will accept homeless, queenless bees as their own. And high in the trees in the forests were a growing number of African hives.

Thus in a matter of a few weeks millions on millions of domestic bees without colonies of their own joined the Africans, swelling their ranks. Thanks to man, the enemy forces became much stronger than B Group had bargained for or realized.

PART FOUR

The
Battle of the Bees

19

THE WASPS

The battle of the bees—"with" is more correct than "of," but "of" is what people said—culminated in late August; by then thousands of encounters and many casualties had occurred, but the outcome was not to be settled until the closing moments of the conflict in the skies over New York City.

For the moment the enemy remained in his base areas, or moved only very slowly. But according to all reports, the African bees were rapidly increasing in number. Buildups such as this one always precede an insect migration. The population grows until nature can no longer support it, and then the mass movement of millions or billions of insects begins. A migration of the African honeybees, such as had already occurred in Brazil, was just what the scientists at Detrick hoped to prevent by reducing the population of hostile bees. The first weapon to be deployed was the so-called "bee cocktail."

Manufactured by Du Pont in Delaware, the cocktail—a blend of aromatic honey, LSD, the insect growth regulator and spores of American foulbrood—was ready on schedule in the third week of May. Hundreds of thousands were dropped by plane over the three bee-infested areas. One small package drifted down in a clearing near Maryville, spreading its honeyed fragrance.

A large black bee with orange tufting appeared, then another, and another, hovering around the cocktail. A bee approached, retreated, approached and retreated again, without tasting the offering. The bees flew away. No one would ever know exactly why. A rational explanation existed: flowers were plentiful and the bees preferred their natural food. Or perhaps the delicate, mandibular sensory apparatus of the bees detected something foreign. Or perhaps . . .

"Reports from bee wardens. Been observing the Africans from a distance through field glasses. They are passing up the cocktail. Don't like it. Maybe we should have added booze," Gerston said.

Wood's solemn face winced in disappointment. "Pray for our queens."

"Goddamn bees," Gerston said bitterly. "Do you suppose they suspect something?"

"General Slater to see you, sir," said the voice on the intercom.

Wood and Slater had talked on the phone, but this was their first meeting since the one at the Pentagon. The general's bulk overflowed one of the folding chairs scattered around the table in the command room. Still reminding Wood of a British sergeant major, Slater asked, "Everything in hand?"

"Hard to say. Preliminary observations conducted by the bee wardens on the cocktail aren't encouraging. The Afros don't seem to like it. Funny, it tested out in the experimental hive," Wood said.

"You should have gone the pesticide route from the beginning," Slater offered. "Our planes could have saturated the areas with DDT or something else. Still can."

"The Environmental Protection Agency won't permit it. I've checked. Besides, what would you get? Pesticide-resistant bees? And we might mess up the ecology for years to come." He pondered, screwing up his lean face, trying to think of terms

Slater would readily understand. "Suppose nature had a second-strike capability, General? Like our missiles. I mean, we keep throwing stuff at her, and after a while, in desperation, she starts fighting back with weapons of her own."

"Like the bees?" The General smiled benignly.

"Well, yes, like the bees," Wood grunted.

"Come, now, what is the word for that? 'Anthro—' "

" 'Anthropomorphism.' I know—it's a fallacy. Just the same, I'm of the school that says we don't know all the laws of nature yet. Anyway, I'm convinced that we should use a pesticide only as a last resort and when we can kill the bees in large concentrations."

"Meaning, around the cities—if they get that far?"

"Yes."

Slater said, "I've been assigned by the Advanced Research Projects Agency to look into this matter. Somebody had the bright idea sophisticated defense might be needed. Me, I'm for issuing a bunch of flyswatters."

"Bee swatters," Wood said. "We've already developed them." He went over to another table and returned with a swatter made of light metal mesh about the size of a squash racquet.

"That ought to do it, God knows," Slater snorted.

Wood sat back. "Well, you'd think so, but it's hard to imagine exactly what we're facing here. Is it a matter of a few colonies terrorizing a neighborhood? A lot more bee stings than usual, and some of them deadly? Or a swarm of hundreds of thousands of bees in an ugly mood pouncing, as the Afros have done in Brazil and here at Maryville? Or . . ." He trailed off.

"Or?"

"Well, I used to dream of bees. I remember one dream where there was this enormous eye—a bee eye, maybe—on top of a stalk. What does a great big eye in the sky suggest to you?"

"Pie in the sky?" Slater said cheerfully.

195

"Not to me," Wood said, ignoring Slater's derision. "It says a whole sky full of bees. Almost like locusts."

"You've got a vivid imagination for a scientist. I think you're still dreaming." Nonetheless he paused for a moment, playing with the metal buttons on his uniform. "Tell me, what sort of characteristics do these bees have that might be used to our advantage?"

Wood made a mental scan of the ethogram. "Let's see. They're attracted to bright lights. That suggests that one defense might be fire. They're usually sensitive to vibrations."

"Would sonic beams disorient them in flight?"

"Maybe. Got one?"

"I'm not at liberty to say." Slater laughed again. "Sonic beams! I keep forgetting we're talking about *bees*. Christ, they're not the Chinese or the Russians."

"You're a hard man to convince, General," Wood said. They began discussing things bees might not like. Wood came up with pollution.

Signs had been posted in bee-infested areas:

WARNING
AVOID BEES
REPORT WILD HIVES

Teams of men and women scoured the woods. These were the "bee wardens," specially trained in killing the dangerous bees. They wore thick outergarments, hats, and facepieces not unlike fencing masks. They carried ladders, field glasses, swatters, and guns that could shoot a small cyanide pellet directly into a hive entrance. But their job was not made easier by the African bees. Reverting to ancient heritage, they built their hives at the tops of trees, where they were hard to spot, much less reach. When a bee tree was spotted, the wardens often had to chop it down. Few African hives were killed by the wardens.

Near Maryville, bee wardens were patrolling the second-growth timber without finding hives. Everywhere normal-looking bees busily foraged in beds of rife wild flowers, ignoring the humans as they darted about, sipping the sweet nectar of flowers. A sleepy hum of insects filled the warm woods. It might as well have been the call of Sirens. One warden, seeing how peaceful it was, lay down for a second, removed the mask from his overheated face, and unbuttoned his shirt. Minutes later he was dead.

At Detrick the MARS facility, operating round the clock, crackled with news of bees, and the results were fed to the computerized map in the control room. The trend was unmistakable: invaders were stepping up the pace.

It was June 1.

Conscious of their absent teammate, Wood, Amaral, Gerston, Fine, McAllister and Krim gathered in the control room in their laboratory smocks. The mood was tense, like that of generals before a campaign.

As usual, Maria began with the pointer. "On the basis of information received in the last few days, it looks as though the Africans have started to swarm."

On the map the change was almost, but not quite, imperceptible. The southern rims of the bee perimeters had extended slightly.

"Time to move," Wood said decisively. "When can we drop the queens?"

"I'd hoped to give them a few more days flying time in the 8-ball," Mac McAllister said. "I guess we can roll now—not that I've a whole lot of faith in this genetic-change stuff."

Krim, however, did. Having started out as a skeptic, the

197

geneticist had swung over. He had become convinced that Project Queen would succeed, but he had no way even to calculate the odds until he could design a mathematical model and run it through the computer. But still there had been no time. "It'll work, I tell you," he rasped angrily.

McAllister shrugged.

"You're all betting on your own horses, naturally," Wood observed. "Walter Krim, here, on the queens, Mac on the workers, Gerston on his drones. I wonder which one, or ones, will prove themselves. It'll be more than interesting to find out. I hope in a couple of weeks we'll be making toasts."

Gerston joked, "Whichever wins, ours are all American bees." He blinked his eyes. "White Anglo-Saxon Protestant bees—WASPs!"

They all laughed, even Krim.

Wood said, "All right. Here comes the WASPs. Godspeed."

The mood in the control room was momentarily optimistic.

Of the three lines, the queens had presented the hardest technical problems. While the other bees could be stored and fed in boxes, the queens needed special handling. During the pupal phase, when they were dormant, the queens were separated and placed in small wire cages, each with a knot for worker bees to feed them. For this operation more human labor had to be employed than with the other lines.

And queens, more than the other castes, must test their wings. Before her nuptial flight a queen takes to the air experimentally to gain strength and experience. A few days after the queens had emerged from pupation they were brought by the thousands to the huge test sphere at Detrick, there to fly, while the Africans were kept in their hives.

One group at a time, the cages were opened, and, cautiously, a fresh queen stepped outside. Her first flight was short—only a few feet. It was soon followed by a second, a third, a fourth, and then the queen circled around the huge sphere to the very top. A queen would always return to the cage from which it had emerged, where its bee family was. The unfailing ability of queens to find their own cages, just as they would find the right hives in nature, never failed to surprise the Detrick scientists.

Now the queens, all theoretically carrying defective genes, were ready. The tiny cages with food inside were packed in lightweight plastic boxes, sent by truck to Andrews Air Force Base and by plane to staging areas where the helicopters waited. The boxes had been carefully designed and tested. They fluttered down, and on impact they shattered and the cages within disintegrated. It was important that the queens no longer had a home to return to.

In search of mates, the queens flew, flooding the air with the sex pheromone. Not all the queens found drones (the ones that failed eventually died), but some entered the zones where drones congregated and were pursued by the hot bee bucks, drawn inexorably by the queen's powerful sexuality and eager to exchange their lives for a single orgasmic spasm that brought both life and death.

One mated queen, the drone's organ torn from his body and protruding from hers, located an African hive. The guard bees, seeing the signs of her pregnancy, let her pass, and she entered the hive uttering her war cry—*seep, seep, seep,* she piped. While she waited, which was not long, worker bees removed the spent tool of the drone from her body. Then over the dim comb marched her adversary, a huge African queen, a black-and-orange Amazon, murderous with rage, flaunting her sting curved like a cutlass.

The queens sprang at each other in fury, each seizing the antenna of the other with her jaws. The head and abdomen of each were exposed for an instant to the head and abdomen of her rival. They had only to deflect the tips of their abdomens and each would have pierced the other with her sting, ending the duel in the death of both. Instead, almost as though this outcome were forbidden, each queen backed off.

They circled warily, jostled by workers insisting that combat continue until one gladiator was dead. The Amazon was big, strong, heavy, but laden with eggs and slow; the "dumb" American deft, agile. Again they grappled, belly to belly, backing off and circling. The worker bees were beginning to crowd them together, which meant almost certain death for the smaller queen in the embrace of the Amazon.

At last the Amazon lunged. Lifting her abdomen, pointing her sting, she struck powerfully—and missed. Momentarily off guard, she was perhaps confused. Quickly the smaller bee seized the head of the Amazon with her mandibles, and the wings and thorax with her legs. She climbed upon the Amazon's body, and suddenly, twisting her own body into a ring, plunged her scimitar into the Amazon again and again. The African queen shuddered, dropped, and was soon dead. The victorious queen lunged this way and that, poison dripping from her weapon, seeking other opponents. Satisfied there were none, she returned her sting to its sheath.

Without ceremony, worker bees hurled the dead queen from the hive. The queen was dead, long live the queen.

Of this the scientists at Detrick knew nothing. They had attempted to introduce a genetic strain of self-destruction into the factory-made queens, hoping they would pass it to the African invaders. But besides being stupid, Henry David's pets had been fierce fighters in their dealings with other bees. At least this part of their heritage had been transferred to the line-reared queens, and it served them well.

The boxes containing worker attack bees tumbled out of HUEY helicopters and fluttered to the ground. When a box struck, a vial containing isopentyl acetate was broken and the alarm pheromone released.

In a much more concentrated form than existed in a hive, it transformed the dazed young workers into a buzzing mob, held together by their chemically induced perception that other bees were trying to rob their honey stores.

If there were no hives in the vicinity, these bees soon became confused and dispirited. If there was a hive around, they attacked it.

Several such boxes landed at the Maryville clearing near the remnants of the useless cocktail. The bees, six thousand to a box, rose, snarling. Above, high in the tree, was an African hive, with guards patrolling the entrance hole.

An army of conscripts against professionals.

The big guards stirred at the approach of the small intruders. Perhaps a few guard bees went down before the onslaught, but then from inside the hive came the awful war chant of the Africans, *ziiiiiiiii*, ZUUUUUUUUMMM—and the outpouring began.

The hive returned to normal. On the ground by the tree were piled the bodies of thousands on thousands of little American bees.

McAllister was livid. "Bee wardens report the worker-bee attack failed. Our troops fell on their faces. No good, no good at all. Why? Why? Why?"

"The Africans are tough," Wood said dispiritedly.

"I hate them—I hate those bees," McAllister shouted, pounding the table.

"Calm down, Mac," Wood warned. "Don't lose your objectivity."

"I don't want to be objective. I want to *kill the bees*."

Perry Goodall, the bee lover, worried about the mounting national intolerance toward bees. He knew about the Africans, of course, but more and more he came to believe that the real enemies were the idiots who urged killing off bees altogether.

They were boycotting honey—so effectively that supermarkets had stopped carrying the product. Just as well, Goodall thought, because there wasn't enough honey to go around.

The kooks claimed that bees were unnecessary for pollination. They said that machines could do the job as well or better. A patent for a pollination machine had already been filed.

Goodall scoffed. As if the machine could replace a worker with hundreds of thousands of years' experience!

What really worried the public-relations man was the Kill-the-Bees Act, now before Congress, which would make beekeeping illegal and the extermination of hymenoptera a national policy.

Goodall decided to act. He announced a rally at Madison Square Garden at which he would offer conclusive proof that domestic bees were still safe. But he refused to reveal the nature of the proof until the actual event.

Dropped exactly the same way as the workers, the sterilized drones rose from the box fresh, fed, and ready for action.

The drones did as drones do—they found congeries of drones and joined them, flying in circles as they waited for a queen's appearance.

A queen came—an African queen—flying high and fast, spreading her scent. The drones rose to meet her.

Her first pass was only flirtation, but the second meant business. Higher and higher drove the queen, with the drones spread out behind her. She looped, turned and twisted as she flew, testing the endurance of the drones. Up, up she went, bent for the blue, and now the weaker drones began falling off, to return to the staging area and wait for another queen.

At 75 feet she wheeled contemptuously, waiting for the band of drones to reach her level; and a few did, among them sterilized drones. But this was no ordinary queen. Again she rose,

wings shimmering in the sunlight, this time to impossible regions, 80, 90, 100, 150 feet above the earth. And there she was
taken—or rather, she took. The mating couple fell slowly in
their airborne nuptials. The stricken drone that left his organ in
the queen's body was a large black bee with orange markings.

Other drones would have her too—all African.

20

DEATHWATCH

After Hubbard's death Fine kept to himself even more than before. He labored endlessly, eating alone and at odd hours. His pallor deepened.

He had recurring thoughts: If he had been a better scientist, the antidote might have been ready and Hubbard's life saved. Or if he hadn't still been angry with Hubbard, he might not have hesitated just that crucial second outside the glass hive; he might have entered and tried to pull the man out. In Fine's mind, as Wood was soon to learn, the rat of guilt gnawed.

Late one night Fine made his decision.

The tests on rhesus monkeys had been a disappointment. One effect the hyped-up venom had was to stiffen the monkeys' musculature. This had serious implications for human beings, because a man who had been stung might have trouble getting the ampule from his pocket and injecting himself. How much and how fast the venom affected human responses was hard to judge from laboratory animals. They couldn't tell you, and even the eight-channel Hewlett-Packard physiograph recorder had no way to measure such a response.

The other problem had to do with sight. Too much proto-atropine seemed to cause a blurring of vision, and even blindness, in experimental animals.

There were, then, practical limits to how much antidote could be administered. The proper dosage fell within a narrow range

—too narrow, conceivably, to work. Given time, Fine might have eliminated the blindness factor from the antidote, but there was no time. Wood was pushing the toxicologist relentlessly. The autoinjector had to be ready for mass distribution, and soon.

Fine had arranged for a convict volunteer, who was now at Fort Detrick under guard. But the trouble was that if Fine waited for the volunteer to use the autoinjector himself, the venom might kill him, and if Fine administered the antidote to the volunteer, the test would not be a true one. There was, in other words, a risk, a risk that Fine, in the end, decided to take himself.

He assembled his notes carefully, stage by stage. He gave exact instructions on obtaining the clearance for the secret chemical, and neatly printed the results of his experiments with the lab animals. He inserted into his notes some remarks about his guilt feelings in the matter of Sheldon Hubbard's death. Then he did something he had not done since boyhood—he prayed.

In the lab was a couch that Fine used when he wanted to rest. He placed the alarm button near it, removed his shirt, pushed over the physiograph, and switched it on. A red light flashed, and the ten-second timer began to click. Satisfied that the equipment was working, he attached the blood-pressure coupling to his upper arm, and then began attaching electrodes to himself with contact fluid and pieces of tape. One went to his temple, another to his rib cage, a third to his upper chest. These leads would give readings on blood pressure and respiration, and would also provide electrocardiograms and electroencephalograms. These four responses would be enough.

Fine hesitated a moment, thinking about the laboratory animals. But he also thought about his wife, and taking a hypodermic needle from the table, he injected himself with the exact quantity of venom he would have received from the stings of five toxic bees—the maximum the antidote could suppress without causing blindness. He watched the weal rise on his skin where the needle had punctured it. Then he turned his attention to the Sanborn vertical recorder, on which the tracings of his responses had begun to appear.

Click, click, click—the timer counted the seconds.

Fine did not have long to wait. Seconds after the injection he saw rather than felt his first response. His blood pressure had dropped slightly. Then the machine informed him that his heart rate was rising, and rapidly. It had begun at 80, but leaped to 120 beats per minute, then 130. His body sent messages to him now: his heart pounded in his chest, he was sweating, and he felt jumpy and tense.

There was a clock on the wall. Approximating the conditions under which a self-injector would be used by an ordinary person, Fine had concluded that, from the moment of a sting, a hurt, frightened, medically inexperienced person would need about 60 seconds to get the injector from pocket or purse, pull up a sleeve, hesitate because of fear of the injector, and finally put the needle in. Fine's heart rate was 140, and he reached for the ampule on the table at 55 seconds.

Oh God, he said to himself, I can't move.

His right arm felt strapped to his side. Only with the greatest effort could he lean forward and, gripping his wrist with his other hand, force his fingers toward the self-injector containing the antidote.

I used too much venom, he thought.

He had the ampule in his hand, but his aim was off. Three times he jabbed and found only empty air. Finally he managed to hook the needle into his flesh, pressed the nipple and injected himself with antidote.

Looking at the physiograph again, Fine realized with alarm that his heartbeat had reached 160, close to the outer limits. It now began to recede . . . 140, 130, 120, 110, 100. His brain waves showed aberration, but his mind was functioning normally as far as he could tell. His respiration was high, but not abnormally so. On a pad he scrawled the exact time at which the antidote had been administered.

The worst is over, his mind said. The antidote works.

It was at this point in the experiment that something happened, or rather, failed to. If the antidote had performed properly, Fine's responses should have returned to normal almost at once. Looking at the tracing, Fine realized that the four physiological responses were hovering on plateaus between normal and alarming levels. They refused to recede.

In fact, they were turning bad. Fine was a man on a physiological roller coaster, and could only watch.

His heart rate rose . . . 120, 130, 140, 150. He felt a sharp pain in his chest. But his eyes were focused on the band recording his respiration, and now George Fine knew that his trouble was mortally serious. He was losing respiration and was gasping for air. With respiration failing, his heart pumped faster, and his EKG became erratic from lack of oxygen. The symptoms pointed as straight as an arrow to a respiratory arrest within minutes.

He had two emergency procedures. One was another dose of antidote, though it meant risking blindness; the second was the emergency button on the wall. The fresh ampule was within easy reach. Fine got it into his fingers and looked at it helplessly— his arm was too weak to move. With his last strength he pushed his shoulder against the button. Outside the lab door a trumpet began to wail through the silent facility.

Wood's personal DEW line had been sending signals to him, and unable to sleep, he heard the trumpet's blast. He reached the lab area first and found the machine still clicking, the pens still moving across the paper, only now the lines they made were straight. Fine was dead—the physiograph left no doubt of that. Wood turned it off and looked at Fine's notes, grasping at a

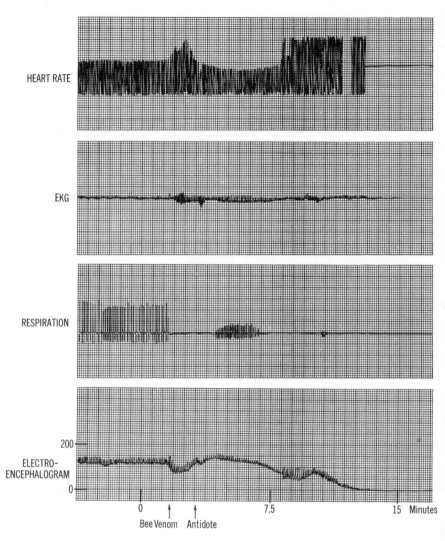

Fig. IV: Dr. Fine's death chart. (Courtesy National Institutes of Health)

glance what had happened. He raged inside—at Fine's needless sacrifice, at the fact of death and at the caprices of chemistry that had decided conclusively there would be no antidote against the sting of toxic bees. There was no time left to develop one.

21

CRACK-UP

Swelled by emerging brood and new arrivals, the hive had become too crowded, even for bees, and now in the superorganism, the colony, a decision was made and transmitted by mass communication. The hive would swarm. Headed by the queen, half the bees of the hive, perhaps 50,000 pioneers, would seek a new home. The bees left behind would wait for a new queen to emerge from their cells, and life in the old hive would continue as before. In perhaps a month, given the bounty of nature during the summer and the fecundity of the queen, the hive would again divide.

Meantime, travel preparations had to be made. The queen stopped laying and grew thinner, lither, in preparation for a long flight. The workers gorged themselves, filling their honey stomachs with a week's supply of food.

Fifty feet over the ground, flying fast, the swarm crossed Maryville. Panic swept the streets below—people ran, cars crashed—but it was soon understood that the bees were ignoring the town as though it did not exist.

Miles later, on top of a hill, the hive finally settled. Fanning out from the branch where the swarm waited in a large ball, scouts checked the availability of water and food. Then they inspected the trees, the ground, an abandoned shack. They returned with their recommendations, which were communicated by means of the waggle dance. These dances provided very precise information not merely about the nature of proposed sites but about how strongly each scout felt regarding his own discovery. For hours the scouts danced, while the hive weighed one proposed site against another, taking into consideration the relative enthusiasm displayed by individual scouts. Just before dusk the decision was made, and the bees moved high into a comfortable old tree. In a month this hive would divide as well.

Other hives were swarming—many of them.

As the bees swarmed, action mounted at the MARS facility, where a half dozen operators were now needed on every shift to take the incoming calls.

"CQ, Fort Detrick, Maryland . . . CQ, Fort Detrick, Maryland. This is Whiskey Six Foxtrot Victor Yankee . . . CQ, Fort Detrick."

"Hello W6FVY. This is Whiskey Three Whiskey Alpha Romeo, Fort Detrick, Maryland."

"W3WAR. I'm Albert Potter of Canby, California. In view of your interest in bees, I thought you'd like to know a couple of swarms passed over my house headed south."

"I read you, W6WVY. Thank you. Goodbye."

"CQ, Fort Detrick, Maryland . . . This is Kilo Nine India Lima X-ray."

"Hello, K9ILX. This is Whiskey Three Whiskey Alpha Romeo, Fort Detrick, Maryland. Where are you, K9ILX?"

"Minocqua, Wisconsin. My name is Mrs. Olga Sheridan, W3WAR. I got the bee bulletin. There are bees flying all over around here. They haven't hurt anybody yet."

"Thank you, K9ILX. Goodbye."

"CQ, Fort Detrick. Whiskey One Hotel Sierra Papa calling from Pittsfield, Massachusetts. Come in, Fort Detrick."

"Okay, W1HSP. What's the trouble?"

"No trouble. I read all this stuff about African bees. Plenty bee swarms moving here, but no trouble. I'm Jonathan Gwenn."

"Thank you, W1HSP."

All this information was absorbed by the computer. A week later the control-room map had changed strikingly.

Present at the meeting were Wood, Maria, Gerston and McAllister. Krim was unaccountably absent. Wood scowled. "Where's that goddamn Krim?" he muttered. "We'll hear from Maria first."

Maria Amaral, like the rest of them, looked exhausted. Two profound shocks on top of weeks of little sleep, fresh air, recreation or exercise had left their marks. She dimmed the lights and went to the map with her pointer, as she had done so often before.

"Something is happening out there, no doubt of it. Hundreds of sightings of swarms have been reported recently to Bee Watch. This is true everywhere in the country, even in the South, but most concentrations are still small, or seem to be. It's the three big ones that must cause the greatest concern. They are spreading fastest."

"How fast?"

"About ten miles a week at this point."

"Any particular direction?" Wood asked, though his eyes told him the answer.

"The heaviest migration is always in a southerly direction. It is this leapfrog phenomenon, of course. A swarm flies and settles. Then another and another. Each moves beyond the place of the one before."

McAllister said, "The bees that are left behind when the hives

211

swarm return to their former strength. The colony swarms again. Then the hive that has already swarmed swarms again. This process is duplicated many thousands of times. It's like a succession of waves moving out. The way I look at it, the bees could quadruple in numbers by the end of the summer if the weather stays hot."

They hated the wonderful weather. It had been perfect for flowers and therefore bees. It meant that the bees' larders were full. They would reproduce faster and swarm more frequently.

"When does that farthest edge reach major cities?" Wood asked.

Maria checked the computer. The readout said:

```
PROJECTED ARRIVAL DATES
AFRICANIZED BEES
NEW YORK OCTOBER 4
CHICAGO OCTOBER 10
SAN FRANCISCO OCTOBER 11
```

Wood said sharply, "What year?"

"This year," Maria said.

They gasped. Wood said with quick bitterness, "It's all going according to plan—the bees' plan."

"We've dropped over a billion bees and a million cocktails with no result," McAllister raged, pounding the table.

Maria said cautiously, "But the bees do not seem to be attacking much. Perhaps we have made them peaceable in some way."

McAllister looked at her with what seemed to be pity. He piped, "Bees are always gentle during a reproductive swarm. As soon as the Africans stop swarming they'll turn vicious once more. It won't be long."

Turning her smooth face away from McAllister as though to hide humiliation, Maria said, "They seem to be avoiding the towns and staying in the rural areas. The only people who have been attacked are farmers."

"That will change too," McAllister said glumly. "If they get into the suburbs they'll attack everybody."

"Or the cities," Gerston said. A throb of fear sounded in his voice. "There will be panic like you never heard of. Imagine—cities that are already explosive jammed with refugees!"

"Let's not have any panic *here*," Wood drawled. He was trying hard to control his anxiety. That the bees had started moving was serious news. He wished momentarily that Shelly Hubbard was there to help keep their spirits up. Even Gerston's courage was faltering.

McAllister cried, "Maybe we ought to look into the notion of the Kill-the-Bees bunch. Sending out a million people to battle the Africans sounds better and better to me."

"Stop it, Mac," Wood said quickly. "It's a dangerous idea in lots of ways, and you know it. The thing to do is to stick to plan and keep dropping. Sheer volume may do it."

McAllister said hotly, "You're kidding yourself. Those goddamn bees of ours—not worth a damn. The workers must have been outmatched, the drones outclassed by those big African fuckers." Wood shot him a warning glance, but McAllister ignored it. "As for the mutated queens, that idea is strictly screwball, just like Krim."

Where the hell is Krim? Wood asked himself.

At that point the tiny geneticist entered the room.

Something Wood had said stuck in Krim's tangled brain: "If only we could prove our plan would succeed, we might be able to head off a full-scale public reaction. I'm frightened of that." Krim was determined to find such proof.

The problem was to show why the dumbness-mutation experiment had a good chance of success. He called this "the probability coefficient of the distribution function of 'dumbness' within elapsed time frameworks, graduated by mass." The mathematics involved would have taken a superior Ph.D. candidate perhaps a year. Krim, a genius, had the solution at the end of seven grinding days.

First Krim had to establish his base lines. He did this by contacting the memory bank at NIH, just as Fine had done.

Working with the computer, he emerged with a reference, an article that had appeared in a Soviet scientific journal in 1957, by one I. Podolsky. The Soviets had conducted much experimental work on bees. The article was called "A Study of Bee Elitism," and had been translated. It was rushed to Krim from the Smithsonian Institution by car.

Although the Russian was clearly trying to square his findings with Communist attitudes toward elitism, the message was clear. Even in the advanced socialism of the hives, about 10 percent of the worker bees at any given time acted as leaders; the queen, of course, was an egg-laying machine, not a decision-maker. The leaders determined what actions a hive took—such as swarming or balling an old queen.

Fine had reasoned that any gene that would drive a bee toward destruction must be ruthlessly dominant; otherwise it could not make itself felt as it had with Henry David's hives. Therefore, if he could introduce the death-wish gene at all, only 10 percent of the bees in a hive would have to have it. Such was the strength of the gene that these bees would necessarily be the leaders.

But how many colonies had to be converted? Because the African colonies, with their strong interhive alarm and defense systems, worked more like a single giant hive, Krim reasoned that a conversion rate of 10 percent of the hives would suffice. The target, then, was 10 percent of the bees in 10 percent of the hives.

That left two variables, time and mass: how long the genetic alteration would take, and the amount of genetic material that would have to be supplied. The time factor involved dispersion, and here Krim relied on what geneticists call gamma distributions. He began with the formula

$$S_0^\infty \, y^{a-1} \, e - y$$

This he converted to

$$Pr(W > w) = \overset{k-1}{\underset{20}{\Sigma}} Pr(X = x) = \overset{k-1}{\underset{20}{\Sigma}} \frac{(aw)^x e^{-iw}}{x!}$$

And this emerged after many formulations as

$$O^2 = M''(o) - y^2 = a(a+1)\beta^2 - a^2\beta^2 = a\beta^2$$

Krim now possessed a theoretical model of the problem, except for the question of mass, which still had to be introduced into the equation. This he deferred, on the ground that time and distribution factors would determine mass. But to determine time and distribution factors he had to convert the equations into integers, in order to convey them to the computer in a manner that the machine would understand. This was what took most of the week.

The computer provided an inch-thick sheaf of computations, summarized by a simple message at the end.

PROGRAM: AFRICAN HIVES WILL ACT ERRATICALLY
IF GENETIC CHANGE OCCURS AMONG 10 PERCENT OF
THE BEES IN A HIVE. IF 10 PERCENT OF THE
AFRICAN HIVES BEHAVE ERRATICALLY, ALL
AFRICAN HIVES CAN BE EXPECTED TO ACT
ERRATICALLY. ASSUMING QUEENS WITH
"DUMBNESS" GENE CONTINUE TO BE DROPPED,
PER SCHEDULE, PROBABILITY FACTOR FOR
SUCCESSFUL OUTCOME OF EXPERIMENT IN TWO
MONTHS IS 50 PERCENT.

It was, then, a fifty-fifty shot—better odds than Krim expected. Shaking with exhaustion and excitement, Krim ran to the meeting. He was very late.

Watching Krim as the geneticist entered the room, Wood caught his breath. Smock rumpled, face deeply lined, Krim looked as though he hadn't slept for a week. His red eyes burned queerly. At that moment Wood knew that Krim was headed for trouble.

Ignoring the young geneticist completely, McAllister continued, "Soon the bees will exist in large numbers throughout the country. We'll have a permanent pest that will change the nature of our society. They'll sting us back to the Stone Age."

"I'm scared of those African sons of bitches too," Gerston admitted. "I have my wife and new baby in New York to think about."

Maria pleaded, "But there's no proof the advance will continue. It could easily slow down."

"Not unless drastic action is taken," McAllister insisted. "More and more I favor sending an army of people into the woods to kill the bees."

"A rabble, you mean," Wood scoffed. "I won't go along with that idea. Our defenses may work yet. We've got to be patient, hold on tight, and keep dropping bees."

Wood, too, had momentarily forgotten Krim. Trembling, the geneticist stood up, waving the papers he carried. "None of you knows what he's talking about," he said in a voice even more garbled than usual. "I have the answer. The mutation has every chance . . . of . . . of . . . of . . ." He trailed off, confused.

"Come on, Walter," Wood said.

McAllister snarled at Krim. "Oh, for God's sake, shut up."

"Success!" Krim screamed at him.

"In a pig's eye!" McAllister sneered.

Wood glared at McAllister, and said to Krim soothingly, "Calm down, Walter. Explain yourself."

Krim attempted to. He was so tired that he had to clutch the table for support. The words streamed out. "Zygote stochastic independence heterozygosis Chebyshëv's inequality moment generating function random variables conditional probability gametogenesis maximum likelihood estimation of parameters coefficient of correlation mutation inbreeding rate of decay factor dominance ratio meiosis environmental pressure sequential probability inbreeding quadratic forms we are now in a position to . . ."

He trailed off and stood there dazed, mouth open, spittle dribbling onto his beard. What had emerged was an incomprehensible jumble.

The others gaped at him, speechless. At last McAllister muttered, "The pipsqueak is crazy."

"Pipsqueak!" Krim's tortured mouth managed to say. He started to cry, and ran from the room.

It took them a half hour to find him in the maze of the facility. Knees locked to his chin in the fetal position, he was curled up near one of the metal shields in the sterilization room as if waiting for somebody to pull the switch and flood the room with gamma radiation. Wood called the hospital while Maria tried to comfort him, but Krim seemed oblivious.

After Krim, heavily sedated, had been led away by uniformed soldiers, Wood returned to the control room and leafed through the thick sheaf of papers. Page after page was covered with columns of numbers—the printout was fully as incomprehensible as Krim's monologue. Wood shook his head. It didn't occur to him to look at the last page, where the computer supplied the answer in simple English.

It was several days before the word of the bees' advance reached the public. Meanwhile the Save-the-Bees Coalition

217

held a rally in the Felt Forum of Madison Square Garden.

The hall was full, with tickets ranging from $5 to $100 for box seats. Even at the latter figure the benefit was worth it, considering the talent assembled to perform—rock groups, famous singers, actors, comedians, politicians, intellectuals—and there would be Perry Goodall's big surprise. The same message was repeated by the speakers, on placards and on buttons:

Save the Bees

"What do we want?" Perry Goodall shouted into the mike.
The answer came: "Save the bees."
"What's good?"
"Saving the bees."
"What's bad?"
"Killing bees."
"Bees give us what?"
"Honey 'n' flowers."
"What do we like?"
"Honey 'n' flowers."
"What do we need?"
"Beeeeeeeeeeeees."

Then, as the audience chanted "Save the bees, save the bees, save the bees," Perry Goodall unveiled his surprise. It was the observation hive from his town house, repopulated with bees from Connecticut. There came a gasp when the audience realized his intention. First he smeared a little honey on his fingers, then on his cheeks. Removing the glass side of the hive, he lowered his face, picked the queen from the hive, and placed her on his cheek. The other bees followed. When Goodall turned to face the audience in triumph he wore a full bee beard.

Perhaps the spotlights frightened the bees, perhaps it was the vibrations of thousands of stomping feet. The picture that appeared on TV sets throughout the land was that of a dead man on the floor.

The audience stampeded. Panic had begun.

The crusade brought hundreds of thousands of citizens from every section of the land. They sought a "final solution" to the problem of the bees.

Wood's word "rabble" was descriptive. Dressed in makeshift protective clothing, carrying whatever weapon they supposed would work—flyswatters, baseball bats, shotguns, kerosene, cans of insecticide, even tennis and badminton rackets—they invaded the African sanctuaries. With them, and lending his prestige, was the eminent entomologist F. W. McAllister.

They scoured the countryside, shinnying up trees, beating the bushes, shoving sticks down holes in the ground. They tried to burn down trees selectively—and since they started only seven major forest fires, it can be said that in this they almost succeeded.

The Kill-the-Bees crusade claimed that 100 million bees perished—a figure most observers thought inflated. Also lost from stings and in fires were over 500 human lives.

Its organizers rated the crusade as so successful that plans were announced for another. This second crusade, in early August, found few bees. The mass migration had begun.

Wood found the somber overture to *Madame Butterfly* playing in the control room so depressing that he asked to have it shut off.

Only three remained from the seven original members of B Group, and they were not happy. The citizen crusade made diverting stories for the media, but the scientists knew that the main—and ominous—result of thousands on thousands of well-meaning people trooping through woodlands with swatters, cyanide guns and torches had been to force the Africans to abscond in search of safer homes. Unlike the mood of a reproductive swarm, which is gentle, an absconding swarm is vicious and aggressive—especially so in the case of African bees. These insects, hurtling through the countryside, left terror and death in their wake.

As shown by the computerized map, the bees were fanning out, occupying areas more than twice as large as they had before. If the advance continued, the bees would soon engulf major cities.

"Projections, please," Wood said to Maria.

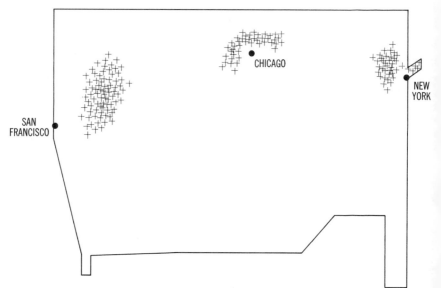

PROJECTED ARRIVAL DATES
AFRICANIZED BEES
NEW YORK SEPTEMBER 4
CHICAGO SEPTEMBER 10
SAN FRANCISCO SEPTEMBER 11

Fig. V: Computer map, August 1. Major concentrations of hostile bees. (Courtesy Apicultural Research and Development Facility, Fort Detrick, Maryland)

CLEVELAND SEPTEMBER 13
DETROIT SEPTEMBER 14
MADISON SEPTEMBER 14
PORTLAND SEPTEMBER 15

"That's enough," Wood said. The screen went blank.

Gerston said in a low voice, "The bees will attack every city in America sooner or later. There's no place to hide."

"So it looks," Wood said dejectedly.

Gerston's big nose was pointed down. He stared at them solemnly. Then he took the photo of his wife and daughter from his wallet and stared at it also, his forehead wrinkling. "I have to think of my family," he said. "I'm getting out."

"You mean out of Detrick?" Maria said.

"I mean out of the United States. This country has had it."

Wood nodded. "I understand. It won't be any fun." He glanced at Maria. "Do you want to go home to South America?"

"I stay with you," she said.

"And you?" Gerston said to Wood.

He answered, "I . . ."—he touched Maria's arm—"we will remain here and continue to direct the drops as long as it's possible. When the Africans get here, Detrick will shut down—but not until then. Call it crazy if you like, but I still believe we have a chance to win."

22

EFFECTS

John Wood and Maria, preoccupied by the bee facility, did not watch the President's speech on television in July. But the President's face was seen by what Nielsen said was the largest audience ever to watch a TV program. He described the rapid spread of the deadly bee across the countryside and the havoc that accompanied it. The voice warned of the impending arrival of African bees in major cities. It urged discipline, courage and resolution. It said that America remained great.

The President then declared a national emergency, and asked Congress to grant him powers such as had existed formerly only in wartime, and in some cases, exceeding even those. There would be rationing of food and gasoline. Industrial workers were told to remain at work no matter what the danger until released from their jobs by the authorities. A corps of bee wardens would be established nationally, and at once, to evacuate people if necessary. Looters would be shot.

The President failed to say what would be done about the bees.

At checkpoints on major highways and rail lines, traffic was stopped and carefully inspected for stowaway clusters of bees, with small result. All over the country African bees were spreading, entrenching, reproducing, swarming again, despite careful search-and-destroy missions to find them.

The first occupation to suffer seriously because of the Africans was farming. African bees made the farmer's life miserable and dangerous. The rumble of heavy machinery, even the smell of sweating men and animals, triggered mass assaults by the rampaging Africans, many of which bore deadly stings. A farmer could protect himself with special gear issued by the Department of Agriculture, but the suits were hot, unwieldy and uncomfortable, and there was no protection for livestock.

Besides, the farmers had their families to think about. Dairy farming stopped first, then the production of pigs, beef cattle, chickens and eggs in many places. Then farming in whole regions, such as the Sacramento Valley in California, ceased under the attacks of hostile bees. The immediate result was a catastrophic rise in food prices, despite price controls and strict rationing.

When the farmers departed, their belongings piled in trucks on top of their cars, they were forced to leave the livestock behind. With no one to tend them, the animals soon died. They would take years to replace. The farmers went to the small towns, but these were quickly besieged by the Africans, and soon a large human population was in flight.

With the towns abandoned, the bee looters appeared. In trucks, wearing headpieces, gloves, and leather jackets decorated with studs or emblazoned with esoteric symbols, they smashed into stores and homes, carrying off anything they wanted. Battles between the roving looters and the army became ever more frequent. In many towns and smaller cities military garrisons were set up. Between the bees and the thugs, the life of a soldier was hell.

Highways, railroad beds, telephone and electric wires began to deteriorate rapidly. Washed-out bridges lay unrepaired. Untended dams were weakening; soon many would burst.

On top of this, industrial production began to decline, first because of a shortage of raw materials, and then because the dangerous bees began to harass ever larger areas. Efforts to keep the men at their jobs failed. In Gary, Indiana, for instance, steel production all but ceased. The stock market, of course, reacted violently. But there were those who professed to see a lesson in all this, because pollution declined as rapidly as production, and soon the air and the streams began to clear.

Optimism was short-lived. In unmanned warehouses, drums containing toxic chemicals began to leak or burst. The chemicals entered the atmosphere or leaked into the streams. The effect on wildlife was catastrophic.

In large sections of the land civilized life was coming to a halt. There were international repercussions too.

As the weeks passed and the Africans continued to progress, causing ever greater turmoil, foreign nations became increasingly dubious about the ability of the United States to control the bees. If Americans couldn't stop insects, our allies reasoned, what protection could they possibly offer against the Russians or the Chinese? Alliances of long standing between the United States and its overseas partners were weakened or ruptured. The North Atlantic Treaty Organization, for one, collapsed.

American goods were still allowed to enter other countries, but inspection procedures became so elaborate that crippling delays ensued, reducing exports and making traveling on American transport a chore.

There was loose talk about an international quarantine, after which the retreat of the dollar turned into a rout. Many insisted that the United States was through as a world power, no matter what the American President said. That, apparently, was the opinion of the United Nations, which commenced a frantic move from New York to Nairobi. The official reason was that the UN ought to be located in a developing country to demonstrate concern and goodwill toward the Third World. Unofficially, however, it was well known that the UN delegates lived in deadly fear of the bees.

Not all the international response was self-interested or unfriendly. Indeed, lend-lease arrangements with the Common Market and the Soviet Union, though the terms were stiff, helped avoid famine in the United States. And a group of East African nations offered technical assistance in fighting the bees. Only Africans, they claimed, had the know-how to deal with African bees.

This offer was harshly refused by the President—too harshly, perhaps, for in Nairobi a debate began in the General Assembly on whether the UN should intervene, even though it meant sending troops against American wishes. Many felt, some Americans among them, that United Nations occupation of the United States was the only way to prevent a great power struggle for control of the ravished land.

The African advance continued. One scheme that reached the President's desk from the Pentagon called for blanketing the nation with thousands of tons of the strongest pesticides. Only a last-minute memo from John Wood, pointing out that the dosage required to kill the African bees would also kill a third of the human population and render huge areas uninhabitable for years to come, prevented the activation of this plan.

Quickly the bees extended their sway, swarming, building hives, swarming and building hives again. Soon they entered the suburbs, which brought them into continual contact with people as the bees foraged in gardens and in garbage cans. The residents began to leave in large numbers, and the White House decided that evacuation procedures should be put into effect and pesticides used in key salients.

One of these salients was Long Island, where an ominous bee buildup had been reported, and among those who had to be asked to evacuate was Mrs. Adele Terrace of Oyster Bay. "I have lived in Oyster Bay since I was born, and I will stay here until I die," Mrs. Terrace told the press. True enough, as it happened—but the effect of Mrs. Terrace's statement was to encourage others to fiercely resist evacuation too, in turn delaying the use of pesticides until it was too late.

For John Wood, soon to be working with General Slater on the defense of the city, the battle of New York would be critical. If the city could not defend itself successfully, neither could the United States.

If the bees could not be destroyed in pitched battle, no area would be safe against them. The following spring they would return, stronger than before, and it might be too late to root them out—ever. Mac McAllister may have helped fulfill his own prophecy by joining those who dispersed the bees, but it seemed possible, even likely, that the bees could destroy the fabric of society, or as McAllister had put it, "sting us back to the Stone Age."

The world watched, and it waited.

23

BEFORE THE BATTLE

It was late August. The air shuttle bringing John and Maria from Washington to New York landed at Kennedy Airport. LaGuardia, where the shuttle normally came, was closed because African bees had been spotted in the immediate vicinity. Kennedy Airport was open only during the day. Airports need beacons and runway lights, and bright flickering lights, as the ethogram indicated, attracted African bees.

The confusion at Kennedy was unimaginable. Thousands of people, desperate to get out of the country, stood at long lines before the ticket counters. They screamed at the harried attendants and waved money. Planes were departing one after the other, after excruciating delays, taking people to Hawaii, Europe, the Caribbean—anywhere to escape the bees.

Wood spotted a tall, familiar figure by the newsstand and walked over. Gerston had come up two days before to get his wife and child, and he, too, was about to leave.

"Where to?" Wood asked him simply.

"Alaska. I figure they won't get there for a while." He looked down at his distant feet. "I want to apologize again. I hate to run out on you, but I don't see that there's much more I can contribute, and, frankly, the safety of my wife and kid comes first, as I said."

"Don't apologize," Wood said soberly. "We do what we have to do."

"Thanks," Gerston answered. "Give Maria a kiss."

One change in the city could be seen as they drove into Manhattan in a chauffeured car operated by Civil Defense. There were plenty of buses but few private cars, which had been banned during the emergency; huge banks of parked cars ringed the city, where the suburban refugees had been compelled to leave them. The air over Queens was clear.

"It's an interesting thing," Wood remarked to Maria as they entered Manhattan, "but this is the closest thing to modern warfare Americans have ever experienced. We've fought abroad, but we don't know wartime conditions as others do. Now we're getting a taste."

He was right. Uniformed men and women wearing Civil Defense armbands and white helmets equipped with wire mesh face shields patrolled the streets. They carried cyanide handguns and large metal swatters. The old shelter signs, returned from retirement, bore the word "Bee" crudely stenciled over "Bomb." Every block had a bee shelter.

The streets were packed with pedestrians. "See how queerly they're dressed!" Maria cried.

Everyone—male and female—wore high shoes and heavy canvas slacks. They wore or carried drab canvas jackets that looked like windbreakers except that they were equipped with hoods. Each person had a kit hanging from his shoulder or from around his waist. It was hot, and the heavy clothing was dark with sweat.

"They look like the Chinese Communists are supposed to look," Wood said dryly.

The car, blowing its horn, was pushing through the pedestrians walking in the streets. Suddenly the sirens blew. Wood tapped the driver and asked him to stop. It was a drill, from which the Civil Defense marking on the car seemed to exempt them. At once wardens appeared. They pushed people into a high-rise building, using their nightsticks like cattle prods.

Others were shoved into a subway entrance, which was equipped with a large metal screen that could be closed.

A woman refused to go into the subway. A warden argued with her.

"You have to go, ma'am. It's for your own good. And it's the law. No one can refuse to take shelter. Read the instructions." He pointed to papers that he carried on a wire loop.

She screamed, "I won't go. I have claustrophobia."

"You have what?" He peered at her jacket, leaned forward and removed a button from under a fold, holding it up. Wood saw that it was a button of the now-defunct Save-the-Bees Coalition. "One of those freaks, eh?" He blew a shrill whistle attached to a cord around his neck.

A policeman arrived instantly. "Now, please don't make trouble, miss. Go along with the others," he said in a tone meant to be placating. Then he saw the button and his voice became openly harsh. "Get inside or I'll arrest you. I ought to arrest you anyway for not carrying your kit. And take my advice—stop wearing that button."

Frowning, Wood called the warden to the car and asked to see an instruction sheet. He and Maria read it together.

NEW YORK CIVIL DEFENSE
INSTRUCTIONS

1. In the event of a bee raid, sirens will blow. Persons on the street—on foot or in vehicles—and persons in dwellings not certified as beeproof are instructed to take shelter in designated areas. Failure to comply is a punishable offense.
2. Drills will occur as deemed necessary. The above provisions will apply.
3. Beeproof areas: subways and department stores; high-rise office buildings; stores built since World War II; residences built since World War II. *Warning: Window glass in structures built before World War II is not necessarily beeproof. Wood shutters in such structures are required.*

229

4. All persons must carry a kit, visible to Civil Defense officials, containing wire face netting, a gas mask, and heavy gloves.
5. All persons are required to comply with the following clothing regulations. All persons, regardless of sex, must wear or carry with them at all times when not within a beeproof area a bee-secure canvas jacket. All persons must wear bee-secure trousers (skirts are expressly forbidden), protective socks and high shoes of strong material. Children must wear the same clothing as adults. Infants must also be protected.
6. Looting during a bee raid or bee drill is severely punishable. The police are instructed to shoot to kill.

OBSERVE THE LAWS—THEY ARE FOR YOUR OWN GOOD

"Gas masks?" Wood said, raising his eyebrows. "They expect to spray the town with cyanide?" He began to laugh.

He looked up to see the warden eying him sternly. The warden said, "You'd better get your gear or you'll be arrested." He strode away.

"Not a very friendly city, is it?" Maria said as they drove off.

But in that she was not entirely correct.

The car stopped at the former UN building, now mostly empty, and Maria went to Bloomingdale's to buy the equipment while John conferred with General Slater.

The army had undertaken the defense of New York. Its headquarters were on the thirty-eighth floor of the building, and the walnut-paneled office Slater occupied had been that of the Secretary General. Wood looked around approvingly.

"It's a step up from the Pentagon, General," he jested.

"Not bad duty, if I do say so," Slater answered. To Wood he seemed leaner, trimmer, as though he'd gotten in shape for a bout. "I never expected to be back in action again. Think we'll see some?"

"Chances look pretty good to me, judging by Detrick."

Appearing in the Frederick area in ever larger numbers, the bees had finally attacked the facility and some had gotten in. The facility had been evacuated and the remaining line-reared bees had been killed. Now the Africans were moving on Washington.

"The computer predicted they'll arrive in the capital about the twenty-fifth of September."

"So it's now or never," Slater said.

Over the floor lay thick black cables attached to TV viewing machines and several microphones at a long table. There was a teletype, and two maps covered whole walls. One was a map of the city and its environs, the other of Long Island. The latter was covered with black pins, which, Wood gathered, signaled bee concentrations.

Slater went to the Long Island map. "That's where the big buildup is. If they come in, it'll be from Long Island. Swarms have been arriving for a month. They fly in over the Sound— they've even been spotted moving at night. In some places you can't walk across a potato field without seeing three or four hives—small ones, to be sure, but representing an awful lot of bees in the aggregate. There must be millions of them out there."

"What do they live on?" Wood asked.

"Well, as you know better than anybody, the weather has been such as to give them fantastic food supplies. Still, there probably isn't enough food for all those bees. They raid garbage dumps and cans and even get into abandoned houses in search of food. The population pressure is what drives them on."

"That's been the experience elsewhere," Wood commented. "The question is how they will move."

"Yes, it's the critical consideration. If they come in more or

231

less one swarm at a time, we can stop them without trouble. If they move together . . ."

"I hope you've planned for that contingency," Wood said quickly.

"Absolutely. Our thinking is predicated on a mass attack by a great many bees. I'm convinced we can take care of them."

"May I hear the final procedures?" He knew the battle plan but not how it would be executed.

Slater crossed the room to the giant map of New York City and its eastern environs. On it had been drawn a series of concentric rings. "A number of forward observation posts have been positioned over Long Island—trucks with the most advanced radar, TV and radio equipment, on a twenty-four-hour alert. If the bees begin to move, we'll know, either through visual sightings or from the radar screens. A large swarm will show up on the screens."

"Okay," Wood said.

"Next the defenses come into play. Helicopters, flying out of MacArthur and LaGuardia, will go into action." Slater pointed to the outer concentric ring. "They'll drop coated metal foil strips over the swarms. They'll set up vibrations in the air; hopefully, the bees' flight patterns will be disrupted."

Wood knew he looked dubious, because Slater said hurriedly, "That's just the opening gun. If they keep coming, the F-111s go into action. They'll be flying out of Kennedy—all fields will be closed to commercial traffic tomorrow at 2400—and Floyd Bennett. The notion is to have them hit the bees at sonic speeds. The sonic boom, the jet exhaust, the jet stream—nothing can survive that."

"You're assuming they'll be high in the air?"

Slater said, "They've been swarming at altitudes of over a hundred feet. The F-111 was designed to come in low. Of course, if the bees make it to the city, the planes won't help, because of the buildings.

"Even so, I think the danger of collision will be high."

"We pay a price for everything we do," Slater said solemnly. Wood could tell the General was enjoying himself; his confidence had returned.

Wood asked, "What next?"

"There won't be a next," Slater answered. "But if there is, we're ready. I mentioned sonic beams once. It's secret, but you may as well know. We've developed a supersonic beam that was meant to confuse the guidance systems of SAM missiles. The machines are in a position on the outskirts of Brooklyn and Queens. They won't kill the bees, but they will disrupt their solar and gravity orientation. We hope they'll dive right into the ground or into buildings."

"After that?"

Slater grinned. "Well, this one was your idea. As of tomorrow at 0700 hours thousands of cars will be moved into position along every major traffic artery. They've been wired so that the ignitions can be turned on by remote control. We'll pollute the bees to death."

"Well, it's something we know how to do," Wood said dryly.

"That ought to be the end," Slater went on. "On the absurdly small chance it isn't, Piper Cubs are waiting at Butler. They will spray a methyl parathion barrier on the far side of the East River."

"Good God," Wood said, "what about the people?"

"They are being evacuated. And then—come over here."

Wood followed the General to the window. Below, an endless row of large barges was being pushed into position up and down the river by tugs. "As a last ditch," Slater said, "the barges will be exploded. They're filled with kerosene. It'll turn the river into a sheet of flame and smoke. That ought to get any survivors."

Wood nodded. "The plan's ingenious, all right."

"It can't fail," Slater said, looking enormously pleased. "But there's one little surprise left. Designed it myself, if I do say so."

233

"What's that?" Wood asked.

"A high-intensity strobe light. It'll be located on the RCA building and surrounded by high-voltage wires. What few bees survive, if any, ought to be drawn to it and to certain death."

"Any danger of blindness to people?"

"Some," Slater admitted. "I think we've got it in hand." He stretched and said expansively, "You've been working hard. Why don't you take the rest of the day off and see the town? You'll find it changed."

That afternoon, feeling foolish in the strange clothing, John and Maria toured the town in the chauffeured car with Civil Defense markings.

Slater was right; the city had changed, and more than its attire.

Harlem, for instance. Harlem was packed with refugees, white refugees who had fled the congestion, the crime and the race problem for suburban sanctuaries and exurban retreats. Now they were back in the city they had left, this time jammed into tenements and derelict buildings four or five to a room, or squatted in tents in Harlem's parks, guarding their silver and china. But, oddly, there was little racial tension or stealing. A spirit of crisis gripped the city, and as happens at such times, humanity unified itself, if only momentarily, in the common defense.

Central Park housed more than 250,000 people—nobody knew for sure how many. They lived in military tents, under army supervision, in camps with hastily erected Quonset huts for mess halls. It was the same in all the city's parks. Millions of people had swarmed into Manhattan from the surrounding areas. There was food enough, but just enough.

Wood asked the driver to stop at a hardware store, where he purchased wooden shutters, and then at a supermarket for food.

234

As he and Maria started to get out, the driver said, "You'll need these." He handed them a packet of food stamps.

The scientists knew about rationing, but isolated at Detrick, they had not been aware how scarce and how expensive were certain foods. The steak available was horsemeat, the eggs powdered. Milk did not seem to exist except in the concentrated form. No fruit. The few half-rotten vegetables offered for sale would have been thrown out in other days. New Yorkers, it appeared, mostly subsisted on canned beans from Puerto Rico and pressed canned meats. There was soft white bread and sugary cake in abundance—evidently flour supplies were good. Maria observed that if the siege continued, vitamin deficiencies would soon appear.

And yet, as they soon learned, New York was surprisingly gay.

The couple had decided to give themselves one night on the town on the grounds that they had it coming after months of confinement at Detrick.

New York was browned out, and the window of the expensive restaurant they chose was covered with a curtain. The place was crowded and festive, like New Year's Eve.

"Feels funny," John said, "to be back in a city, sitting in a restaurant, having a cocktail. I'd just about forgotten such things existed. I'd come to think of Detrick as my home. I feel odd, like an immigrant."

"It is certainly strange to be in a chic restaurant wearing *this*," Maria answered, touching her canvas jacket. She glanced at two women sitting at the next table wearing the very same jackets. "At least I'm not alone."

"A toast," John said, looking into the black eyes across from him. "For just one night let's not talk about the bees."

But there was no way to ignore the bees.

The restaurant had a full menu, and Wood asked the captain

where the incredibly expensive meats and vegetables came from. From Europe, the captain said, with a curious glance, on special flights for restaurants. They ordered, and John said to Maria, "Well, eat up. All airports around New York will be shut down tomorrow. No more restaurants."

He said this too loudly. The next table overheard the remark.

Two couples sat there—the men older, in canvas jackets; the women young, their jackets unzipped. They seemed a little drunk, and one of the girls, a blonde who had been staring at John's straight profile, said, "Is it true? No more flights out of New York?"

John said quickly, "That's the rumor I heard."

One of the men scoffed, "Everything's a rumor. What can you believe anymore? Are the bees coming, or aren't they?"

"The stock market says they're coming," said the other man. "It went down another forty points today. It's like 'twenty-nine."

John saw a newspaper on a seat and asked to borrow it. One word shot out at him—"Terrace." The headline said:

MRS. TERRACE KILLED BY LOOTERS
KB Founder Refused to Evacuate

John returned the paper. He said to Maria, "How ironic it is."

The first man was saying, "If the goddamned bees are coming, I wish to hell they'd get it over with. This waiting gets me down."

The dark-haired girl said, "You can still get out. When they block the roads with cars tomorrow, you won't be able to, at least by road."

"Where would I go? It's the same everywhere—bees and more bees." He shrugged. "I should have gone to Europe, maybe. Now it's too late—if he's right about the airports."

He looked at John, who responded with curiosity, "Why haven't you gotten out already?"

The older man said simply, "I wasn't going to be pushed around by a bug. Dumb, huh? It's true of all of us."

The blond girl raised her arms and stretched. The canvas jacket fell open, revealing most of her bare breasts. She did not appear in the least embarrassed. "The way I look at it," she said, "the bees are giving us what we deserve. We have a shitty society, and they've come to zing us for it."

"Come on," said the brunette. "You sound exactly like the bee freaks."

Maria asked, "What is a bee freak?"

The older man said, regarding Maria with interest, "Where have *you* been?"

"Away."

"Well, the bee freaks emerged out of the Krishnamurti nuts. They say the bees were sent by God, who's black, to punish America for its selfishness. It's the limit."

John had been to this restaurant before. It had never had dancing, but now a small combo began to play and, squealing merrily, people started to dance.

Maria smiled. "You people still seem to have fun," she said.

The older man answered, "It's all we have left. Come on, drink up, and we'll have another round. Waiter! Another. For them too." He indicated John and Maria.

"What are you drinking, sir?"

"Why, what else?" the man chuckled. "Stingers, of course."

"Stingers!" Maria shrieked. "Stingers!" They laughed until they had to put their heads on the table. They laughed and they cried. The long months of tension streamed out of them.

Later that night John and Maria stood on the West Side terrace again, as they had on their first evening. The curtained city was quiet. On the streets below nothing moved.

Central Park, filled with the huddled shapes of tents, looked like an army before a battle.

He put his arms around her. "Perhaps this isn't the time to talk about it, but after everything calms down, I'd like to plan a honeymoon. That is, if we get out of this alive."

She looked at him, somewhat shocked. "You doubt that we will?"

"I think there's a chance that we won't. Are you sorry we didn't leave, like Gerston?"

"No." There was silence.

"You haven't answered me, Maria."

"I know."

"Still upset because of my old days at Detrick?"

"I guess so. It changed my picture of you. I mean, we're supposed to be scientists, not killers. We're supposed to work for the good of man."

"Scientists are no different from anybody else," he said uncomfortably. "Anyway, I know now that what we did at Fort Detrick in biological warfare was wrong."

She looked up sharply. "Yes?"

"But not the way you think. It isn't wrong to try to defend yourself in any way you have to. What's wrong is to forget we're not the only living things on the globe."

The bright black eyes were gleaming. "Let's go inside," she murmured urgently. "And let us try to come out of this alive."

24

THE BATTLE OF NEW YORK

Two days later, at 6:55 in the morning, the telephone rang by the bed. Wood picked it up. A male voice said tersely, "It's started. A staff car will pick you up in fifteen minutes, sir."

It was August 31. The Africans were four days ahead of the Detrick computer's schedule.

Maria made coffee hastily while Wood dressed. At seven o'clock he could hear the noise of trumpets from Central Park, rousing the refugees.

Slater's large office had become bedlam as technicians hurriedly tested the equipment, checking leads, twisting buttons, and adding mikes and TV screens.

Wood glanced out the window. On the Queensborough Bridge he could see an endless line of brown army trucks bringing still more refugees into the city. Slater entered the room and came over. Wood said, "Is there a situation report?"

Slater answered, "They must have started moving last night. All over Long Island bee swarms are in the air, heading in this direction."

A voice came in so strongly over the loudspeaker that both men jumped. "This is Signal Corps Communications Van Seventy-two to HQ. Can you hear me?"

"Loud and clear, Seventy-two," said the operator.

"Something's coming," the voice said.

"Where is Van Seventy-two?" Slater called to a man at the map.

"Near Islip."

"How far is Van Seventy-two?"

"Approximately forty miles."

Slater said to Wood, "Can bees fly forty miles?"

Wood said, "I'm afraid these bees can."

Slater went to a mike and pressed the talk button. "Van Seventy-two, this is General Slater. Come in."

"I'm here, sir."

"What do you see?"

"I'm on a hill, sir. I can see what looks like a gray cloud coming this way. I'm looking through field glasses. Maybe it's only a cloud, sir. It *must* be a cloud, it's so big. . . . Here it comes. No, *those are bees!* Jesus, sir, I've never seen anything like it. It takes my breath away. You can't imagine it. The sky is black from one end of the horizon to the other. Jesus, look at it. They cover the sun! It's like an eclipse, they're so thick. Here they are!"

Slater shouted, interrupting him. *"Give us the video, Seventy-two."*

"I'm trying, sir. We're having trouble with the camera."

"Got a reading on speed?"

"Yes. The swarm, if I can call it that, is moving at ten miles per hour. It's bucking a head wind."

"How high is it?"

"The best reading I can give you is that it ranges from sixty to a hundred and ten feet in altitude."

"You mean the swarm is fifty feet thick?"

"That's what the sonar-radar says."

Slater said to Wood, "Good God. That's unimaginable."

Van 72 came in again. "We've got video for you now."

The picture was hazy, but it left nothing to the imagination. Heading toward New York was a wall of bees.

Wood said, "Let's try to get some idea of the size of the swarm."

The operator began checking other Signal Corps vans in the area. It was quickly decided that the bee swarm was two miles wide, one-quarter mile long, and fifty feet deep.

Slater said in a shocked voice, "That must represent every bee on Long Island."

Wood said, almost in a whisper, "And Connecticut and who knows where else. They must have been infiltrating to Long Island in the last few days in unbelievable numbers. There are billions of them."

"Jesus," Slater said. He seemed stunned.

Wood said, "Let's get them."

The helicopters were airborne from LaGuardia in minutes, heading for the swarm. Other helicopters had been assigned the job of camera planes, and with their equipment they flanked the swarm like cowboys herding cattle. The men in Slater's office had a good view of the swarm. It moved slowly but implacably, never changing either altitude or direction, progressing always toward New York.

It was now 8 A.M. If the swarm did not stop, it would reach Times Square almost exactly at high noon.

Dozens of helicopters went into battle, dropping millions of pieces of twisted foil, which looked on the cameras like ordinary TV snow. One helicopter camera located in front of the advancing swarm recorded exactly what happened. The swarm was like an ocean wave. The wave of bees rose and fell, rose and fell, then continued as before.

Slater looked disappointed. He barked an order. Thirty-two seconds later the first F-111 fighter left the runway at Kennedy.

It had been feared that if the helicopters entered the bee stream, the insects would soon clog the intakes and delicate valves. No such problem existed with the fighters. Because of the speed of the hurtling F-111s, air piled up in front of them, pushing flying objects out of the way. In minutes the first F-111 reached the swarm and entered it, traveling at 750 miles an hour, drilling a tunnel into the wave of bees. Where bees had been, there was, momentarily, just a hole. Slater smiled for the first time that morning.

Another F-111 hit the swarm, then another. On the ground, buildings collapsed under the shock waves. The noise, even filtered through the sound equipment, was deafening. Cheer pervaded the headquarters, but not for long. *The swarm began to descend.*

At exactly the same speed and in precisely the same direction, the swarm now moved just above the earth's surface. But its configuration had changed. Ground observers reported it to be some two miles wide, twenty-five feet in thickness, and a half mile long.

Above it the F-111s wheeled angrily. It was possible for the planes to fly this low, but dangerous because of the buildings. Nonetheless several pilots requested and received permission to try. When the second plane crashed, Slater terminated the mission.

At this point something happened for which Slater and Wood had not bargained; had they known in advance, the complexion of the battle might well have changed. At 10:30 A.M. the advance ceased abruptly, as though a signal had been given.

"I don't get it," Slater said.

"Where are they?" Wood asked.

One of the radio crew said, "Hempstead. Hempstead Lake, to be precise."

"Let's have an overhead angle," Wood ordered.

The camera showed the surface of the lake, dark with bees.

Wood said, "There's your answer. They're watering and resting." He snapped his fingers. "Here's our chance. Poison? No, it'll take too long. A bomb! Drop a bomb!"

Fifteen minutes later a fighter-bomber streaked from the

runway at Maguire Air Force Base in New Jersey. It arrived moments late. The swarm had resumed its journey.

Quietly, seemingly peaceful as a cloud, the swarm floated gracefully, casting an enormous shadow beneath it. The front edge of this shadow was approaching the city limits.

"There's something majestic about them," Wood said, watching the spectacle on the screen. "If it weren't so awful, it would be almost beautiful."

"But it *is* awful," Slater said. "I'm activating the sonic beams."

These weapons, mounted on flatbed trucks, began zeroing in on the swarm, pelting it with supersonic beams. And perhaps some disoriented bees did crash into the ground or buildings; but what happened was best illustrated by the movement of the beam, forward, overhead, and then aimed at the swarm's rear, which disappeared into New York. Like the beams themselves, the effect upon the swarm was invisible.

On every major roadway in Brooklyn and Queens the engines of thousands and thousands of parked cars had already roared to life, sending thick clouds of exhaust fumes high into the air. Dead bees by the thousands quickly littered the cars and the ground—with no discernible difference. There were just too many bees. Methodically, the swarm continued on its way.

One of Wood's jobs at this point was to see that the Piper Cubs releasing pesticide did not stray over the crowded streets of Manhattan but remained on the east side of the river, which had been evacuated. The sprayed area would be uninhabitable for weeks. Tensely he talked back and forth with air controllers. The task proceeded without accident. A white mist of methyl parathion now separated Manhattan from the bees like a deadly curtain.

The bees were still an oblong column, two miles wide and a half mile long. All conversation ceased in the big room on the top floor of the former site of the United Nations. Every eye was fixed on the camera carried by the helicopter flying at a safe distance in front of the poisonous white sheet.

The color TV picture at the critical moment was stunningly clear, and Wood understood at once. The white mist began to darken imperceptibly, becoming gray, then solid black. The swarm was coming through. The Africans were ignoring the pesticide!

Slater sat with his head in his hands, while Wood looked out the window. The radio was quiet, the military TV set blank. The men waited in silence. Only one line, represented by the last defense perimeter on the map, stood between Manhattan and the bees, and in Wood's estimation this system was undependable.

On the thirty-eighth floor the roar of exploding barges could be heard through the thick plate-glass windows. Staring down, Wood saw a river of flame ignite, shooting fiery tongues fifty feet into the air, and billows of smoke higher than the UN building itself. The room dimmed, as though it were night. Outside was a bank of smoke. Wood peered through the window with desperate curiosity.

"What's going on?" Slater asked without raising his head.

"Air draft," Wood said quietly. "Hot air goes up."

"What in blazes do you mean?" Slater came to the window.

Wood pointed. At first he had thought the spots were specks of ash. Then he realized the spots were moving. The bees had entered Manhattan. They were clustered on the windows of the UN building, just outside. In the city, sirens began to bray.

If Wood had any occasion for irony in the coming days it was because of Slater's strobe light.

On top of the RCA building, the giant strobe light, with its incredible intensity, was a continual hazard to public health. Two dozen people who had had the misfortune to stare at it as though hypnotized had been blinded for life. Others suffered serious impairment of vision. But not the bees.

The strobe light may have attracted the swarm to the Central Park area, but having arrived there, it found exactly what it was looking for—water in the lakes and reservoir. Bees can carry a week's supply of food, but they need water, and Slater unwittingly had helped them out. Bright, flickering light seemed to interest them no longer.

Then the bees settled on the buildings around the park as though they were giant trees. Wood, who had raced back from the UN building to be with Maria, could hear the faint rattle on his tenth-story windows. Cautiously he opened the wood shutters a crack and at once saw the reason. Big bees were flying against the windows trying to get in. They seemed to see him and pounded harder.

Frightened, but convinced that the glass would hold, Wood opened the shutter a little wider and peered out. Through the crawling black bodies he caught a glimpse of the GM building, its once-gleaming front now dark with bees.

The occupation of New York had begun.

There had been casualties at once.

Almost in a holiday mood, a crowd lined the walkways of the East River to watch the destruction of the surviving bees in the flames and smoke from the exploding barges. Many simply did not believe any bees would make it through the elaborate military defenses, and regarded the precautions taken by Civil Defense as frivolous. Despite the law, these people did not bother with protective gear.

The draft of hot air pushed up the swarm, but the bees, once they were through the barrier, suddenly dropped—hot, furious bees. With no warning at all they fell on the crowd like hot cinders. *Ziiiiiiii*. Many people were fatally stung.

245

Watered and rested, the bees reconnoitered the city in search of food, leaving early and returning late, as they did in their hives. Although enough bees remained in other sections of the city to make life hazardous there too, the main body appeared to regard Central Park as home, perhaps because of the water. They remained concentrated there, to the great anxiety of the refugees huddled in tents and facing almost certain starvation if the occupation did not soon end.

In their search for food the bees were rewarded. Uncollected garbage waited like a feast. Because of American dietary customs, sugar abounded. Pollen proved no trouble for the bees, either, if they needed it, for flour has long been fed to bees as a pollen substitute, and plenty of old bread and cake lay in the garbage cans.

Army headquarters remained open in a desultory way, but Wood stayed in the apartment. He kept in touch with Slater by phone, until, on the second day, phones ceased working when operators refused to appear. But there was nothing Wood or anyone else could do. No one went out unless he was compelled; even if the protective clothing was safe, to have a cloud of bees flying at your facepiece, jabbing at your clothing, was unnerving at the least. And returning home, there was always the chance that toxic bees would slip in at the door. John and Maria stayed in their apartment listening to developments on television. They were marooned in the middle of New York.

One by one, vital services collapsed.

On the second day public transportation stopped and so did taxicabs. Motormen and drivers claimed they could not see well enough through wire masks.

Attempts at maintaining health care were mostly abandoned. Doctors and ambulances made no more calls; hospitals developed elaborate safety procedures, but even so, many patients were stung in their beds. In an old people's home a senile woman left her window open, and not a single survivor was reported.

That there was no mail was the least of New York's worries.

Much more fearsome was the threat of cholera when water-purification crews stopped functioning after being repeatedly attacked by bees.

Electrical service was maintained, but barely. The mayor, appearing on television, forbade use of any electricity beyond that absolutely necessary. Most people complied, though it meant sitting behind closed windows on hot days without air-conditioners.

Perhaps the most unfortunate victims of the bees were the poor.

The bees could shatter old, thin glass, and many poor people had no shutters. Crawling on the windowpanes, a bee, searching for food, might find a chink in the frame or the caulking, or a break in the glass, or a hole that had not been plugged. Letting in even one could be fatal. You could not huddle in a closet forever, or perhaps the protective gear was unreachable, or perhaps, if there were a half dozen children, there might not be time to get them garbed. Again and again panic brought people racing to the streets. The waiting bees did the rest.

New Yorkers existed as isolated units, cut off from one another by the bees, atomized and alone.

Maria asked the question everyone asked. "How long can the bees last?"

John said, "They can carry a week's supply of food, but they must be finding more. It's conceivable that they could stay until the cold weather comes, which might be a month."

Maria shuddered. "We'll starve."

"There will be some food on the convoys," John reminded her. "I'm afraid of no water or electricity."

"There's something else that worries me. Going crazy," she muttered. "My God, it's stuffy in here."

In this fashion the city wound down, amid rotting garbage and heat, under the threat of pestilence, thirst, mass suicide, and eventually famine, while the bees waited. Nor would other cities be able to provide help, for the bees were approaching them as well. To many, it seemed that the end was near. Then, on the morning of the fifth day, something happened.

The first change noted by John Wood, covered with sweat and sitting morosely in the dark, unbearably hot living room, was the silence. He had become so accustomed to the constant rattle of bees striking the windowpanes that the sudden quiet startled him. Inching back the shutters, he saw that the panes were free of bees. He pulled the shutters wide. There were no bees, and none were flying around the window either. He jerked up the casement rapidly, taking great gulps of fresh air, feeling the fresh breeze against his skin. Then he saw. Over the park the swarm had begun to assemble.

He called Maria, and, excited but cautious, they stepped outside onto the terrace for the first time in five days. From every direction bees scudded over buildings, joining the swarm that hovered above the park. Like a collapsing wall, a sheet of bees detached itself from the GM building and floated toward the gathering swarm, so large by now that it seemed to extend from one end of the park to the other.

The swarm rose and fell, as though restless and indecisive. It was making a noise, a deep-throated note, almost a roar—almost, it seemed to Wood, a chant. As a scientist he had been trained not to impute human feelings to the animal world, and yet he could not help thinking that the sound of the swarm was almost unbearably sad.

Then, as they watched, the fantastic carpet of bees began to rise, slowly, powerfully, majestically. From the military tents in the park figures poured, looking up, pointing. People began to run from the buildings, gesticulating, cheering hysterically, watching as the swarm, graceful as a feather, began to move.

Heading south, it floated easily over the tall structures facing the park, sailing past the RCA building, whose strobe light, flickering in empty menace, affected it no more than would a burning match. Then it vanished from their sight. Maria went in and hurriedly turned on the radio.

"I can see them from here on the Empire State building. Yes, here they come. What a sight! My God, they seem to cover half the city. A blanket of bees! They are below me now—I can't see the streets through the bees. It's as if they were solid, there are so many of them. I wonder where they're going. They are still moving, they are not turning back. They are not turning back. Come in, downtown."

"This is Chris Watson at the World Trade Center. We've been staked out here hoping something like this might happen. It's about all there was to hope for, right? I can see them now through my field glasses. Here they come. They are heading straight toward me. How gracefully the swarm flies! I don't know where they're going, but we may be in for a miracle, ladies and gentlemen, and a miracle is what we need. The front edge of the swarm is passing now, to the east of me, heading toward the Battery. I don't know what their objective is, but you folks on Staten Island and in New Jersey better batten down, because they're aimed in your direction. They are not turning back. They are not turning back! . . . They're over the water, moving fast. The end of the swarm is passing below me, the front edge is almost to the Statue of Liberty! They're overflying that too. *Where are they headed?* It looks to me like the Verrazano Bridge. Beyond that—I hardly dare to say it—but beyond that is the open sea!"

Observers at the Narrows, where the Upper Bay meets the

Atlantic Ocean, had the last clear view of the bees. It was foggy at sea, and the hastily summoned helicopters soon lost sight of the bees in the mist. But one thing was known: the swarm was over the ocean.

On the terrace, John and Maria hugged each other. Maria's cheeks were wet with tears. "Did we win? Did poor little Krim's transplant really take?"

He shook his head. "I have this funny, unscientific feeling that the bees could have won if they'd wanted to." In a moment he said, "There's one thing more."

"What?"

"If the bees did it once, they could do it again. I don't want a rematch."

EPILOGUE

Delayed by the national reconstruction until January, the next annual meeting of the American Entomological Association took place once again at the Hilton Hotel in New York, with thousands of scientists eager to discuss the bee invasion turned away for lack of space. It was vital to understand the fate of the enemy in order to be sure that human intervention had been effective.

Like the rest of the country, New York was returning gradually to normal. Industrial production had been resumed everywhere, and the nation's economy was creeping slowly back to pre-bee levels. Food continued to be short—red meat was absent from the banquet tables in the Grand Ballroom. Livestock could not quickly be replaced, and the fall harvest had been meager. But, as the entomologists pointed out, the Africans had left behind a magnificent bequest. Such was the pollination that must have been wrought by the army of bees that crops and flowers would grow the following spring in an abundance never known before.

New bees were being imported from Europe—selected with the greatest care.

At the meeting, interest centered on what had caused the Africans to act as they did. Almost simultaneously with the disappearance of the swarm over New York, all other Africans had flown to water—the sea, lakes, rivers, even reservoirs—and drowned there. It was as though the bees carried a self-destructive mechanism set to go off at the same time.

But why?

Every scientist present seemed to have a theory. Some held that the bees, like dinosaurs, had simply become too big to live. Others had complicated ideas about psychological stress factors. It was already known that bees could die from too much stress, and now some claimed that the extensive patrolling of the invaders, the disappearance of monogyny—rule by a single queen —from the mass swarms, or the difficulty of preparing for winter at such a late date had made the bees functionally neurotic and suicidal. But the main body of opinion held that Walter Krim's work was responsible.

The survivors of B Group entered the ballroom together. Krim was strapped in a wheelchair pushed by F. W. McAllister. He had received numerous accolades and awards, but of all the deserts of his labors none was sweeter than the humble personal apology delivered by the high-voiced entomologist from Kansas University. With them were Gerston, Maria Amaral and John Wood. The ballroom thundered with applause. Krim, though recovering, was still inarticulate, and John Wood went to the podium instead. Carefully he reviewed Krim's work, starting with the discovery of Henry David's "dumb" bees and Krim's brilliant assumption that the strange behavior of these bees was really symptomatic of an underlying, virus-induced genetic defect of a broader kind. Krim had succeeded in straining out the defective genetic substance and in transmitting it to the cells of the factory-bred queens. These insects had mated with African drones, and their offspring carried a new genetic strain both strongly dominant and lethal, as Krim's calculations had predicted. In three generations, perhaps only two, this gene, carrying its message to the Africans, dictated negative survival,

252

meaning death. It had affected the African elite, which had led the bees to race suicide.

Still, as Wood told his hushed audience, Walter Krim's calculations had shown a 50 percent chance of failure. They had been lucky that the coin fell on the right side.

Later that evening John Wood voiced a different possibility. Standing on the terrace with his Brazilian bride, he spoke, as he had once before, of man's craving for certainty. People demand answers, and Krim's answer was the best they had. But, Wood said, smiling grimly in the darkness, perhaps science had no answer.

GLOSSARY*

Alarm-defense system. Defensive behavior which also functions as an alarm-signaling device within the colony. Examples include the use by certain ant species of chemical defensive secretions that double as alarm pheromones.

Alarm pheromones. A chemical substance exchanged among members of the same species that induces a state of alertness or alarm in the face of a common threat.

Altruism. Self-destructive behavior performed for the benefit of others.

Apiary. A place where honeybees are kept. Specifically, a group of hives.

Brood cell. A special chamber or pocket built to house immature stages.

Colony. A group of individuals, other than a single mated pair, which constructs nests or rears offspring in a cooperative manner.

Elite. Referring to a colony member displaying greater than average initiative and activity.

Eusocial. Applied to the condition or to the group possessing it in which individuals display all of the following three traits: cooperation in caring for the young; reproductive division of labor, with more or less sterile individuals working in behalf of individuals engaged in reproduction; and overlap of at least two generations of life stages capable of contributing to colony labor. This is the formal equivalent of the expressions "truly social" or "higher social," which are commonly used with less exact meaning.

Group effect. An alteration in behavior or physiology within a species brought about by signals that are directed in neither space nor time. A simple example is social facilitation, in which there is an increase of an activity merely from the sight or sound (or other form of stimulation) coming from other individuals engaged in the same activity.

Homeostasis. The maintenance of a steady state, especially a physio-

* From Edward O. Wilson, *The Insect Societies* (Cambridge, Mass.: Belknap Press of Harvard University Press, 1971).

logical or social steady state, by means of self-regulation through internal feedback responses.

Honeybee. A member of the genus *Apis.* Unless qualified otherwise, a honeybee is more particularly a member of the domestic species *A. mellifera,* and the term is usually applied to the worker caste.

Insect sociology (insect sociobiology). The study of social behavior and population characteristics related to social behavior in insects.

Mass communication. The transfer of information among groups of individuals of a kind that cannot be transmitted from a single individual to another. Examples include the spatial organization of army ant raids, the regulation of numbers of worker ants on odor trails, and certain aspects of the thermoregulation of nests.

Melittology. The scientific study of bees.

Monogyny. The existence of only one functional queen in the nest (opposed to polygyny).

Odor trail. A chemical trace laid down by one insect and followed by another. The odorous material is referred to either as the trail pheromone or the trail substance.

Patrolling. The act of investigating the nest interior. Worker honeybees are especially active in patrolling and are thereby quick to respond as a group to contingencies when they arise in the nest.

Pheromone. A chemical substance, usually a glandular secretion, which is used in communication within a species. One individual releases the material as a signal and another responds after tasting or smelling it.

Piping. The sound emitted by young honeybee queens after their emergence. It induces return calls ("quacking") from other virgin queens still in the royal cells and stimulates swarming behavior by the workers.

Propolis. A collective term for the resins and waxes collected by bees and brought to their nests for use in construction and in sealing fissures in the nest wall.

Queen control. The inhibitory influence of the queen on the reproductive activities of the workers and other queens.

Superorganism. Any colony, such as the colony of eusocial insect species, possessing features of organization analogous to the physiological properties of a single organism. The insect colony, for example, is divided into reproductive castes (analogous to gonads) and worker castes (analogous to somatic tissue); it may exchange nutrients by trophallaxis (exchange of liquid among colony members), analogous to the circulatory system, and so forth.

Swarming. In honeybees, the normal method of colony reproduction, in which the queen and a large number of workers depart suddenly from the parental nest and fly to some exposed site. There they cluster while scout workers fly in search of a suitable new nest cavity.

255

Waggle dance. The dance whereby workers of various species of honey-bees (genus *Apis*) communicate the location of food finds and new nest sites. The dance is basically a runthrough of a figure-eight pattern, with the middle, transverse line of the eight containing the information about the direction and distance of the target.